How to Get **RICH** Selling Insurance and Annuities to Women!

ADVANCE PRAISE

If men are from Mars and women are from Venus, then Rebecca and Marti are the distinguished ambassadors who can show the men of the planet how to better communicate with woman in their language. I love their book!

Robert A. Kerzner, CLU, ChFC
President & CEO
LIMRA International

This book makes just the right pitch—with literally hundreds of great tips and tools, Rebecca and Marti have described perfectly what sales professionals need to do to be successful. It's a playbook for every sales person who comes in contact with women buyers.

Frank Murphy
Partner
Hunton and Williams LLP

With profound insights and practical tools, Rebecca and Marti provide the savvy salesperson with everything necessary to sell effectively to women. This book is a must-have, must-read manual.

John B. Sullivan
President
Portland Global Advisors, LLC

Maddox and Smye— are synonymous with how best to sell to women in many industries. They have just released their latest book for the financial services industry, and in my opinion, this is the best one yet. This respected and accomplished team generates enthusiasm and develops savvy sales professionals who can and do sell more to women.

Jennifer Berlin
Corporate Vice President
LIMRA International

The How to Get Rich Selling to Women *series is informative and full of content. This book is a fast, easy read, but don't be deceived, the concepts are substantive. It serves as a practical, useful and easy-to-understand guide in selling insurance services to women.*

Martin J. Geller
CEO and Founder
Geller & Company

Rebecca Maddox and Marti Smye in How to Get Rich Selling Insurance to Women *have done for the insurance industry what John Gray did for relationships in* Men are from Mars, Women are from Venus. *This is a must read for a cutting edge sales force — men and women alike, who are interested in setting and obtaining their target sales goals. The antidotes illustrate the sensitivities and sensibilities in successfully selling insurance to today's modern woman.*

Gina Osti
President
Portland Global Advisors, LLC

How to Get RICH Selling Insurance and Annuities to Women!

REBECCA MADDOX, MBA, CPA

MARTI SMYE, PhD

Maddox Smye LLC
Naples, Florida

Published by:
Maddox Smye LLC
300 Fifth Avenue South, Suite 101
Naples, Florida 34102
www.maddoxsmye.com

Literary Agent:
Albert Zuckerman
Writers House
21 West 26th Street
New York, New York 10010

ISBN 0-9727637-2-4

PRINTED IN THE UNITED STATES OF AMERICA
10 9 8 7 6 5 4 3 2 1

CONTENTS

ACKNOWLEDGMENTS

From Rebecca...

Here's a confession...I never wanted to be a salesperson—ever. Growing up in Ohio, daughter of Dan Maddox, a Nabisco salesman, I didn't think being in sales was a "real" profession. In my kid-view of the world, if you weren't a doctor, a lawyer, or a banker, you didn't have a real job. Almost any other career seemed infinitely more important than sales.

Time, age and wisdom change many things—including perception.

Fortunately, in my view and in public opinion, the sales profession is gaining the respect it so seriously deserves. All successful people are in sales—first and most importantly, selling themselves. You simply can't "win" in life if you don't know the basics of selling. In sales, you make things happen. You serve other people—saving them time and money and meeting their needs and desires—through the services and products you offer. I salute the dynamic men and women who have distinguished themselves as leaders in a field that transcends every other profession.

So here I am in sales, like my Dad. I've spent most of my life in corporate America selling in one form or another. Now, as an entrepreneur and business owner, I use my sales ability daily to persuade people to believe in me and the products and services of Maddox Smye. Thanks, Dad, for pursuing a sales vocation and demonstrating daily that serving other people is the truly the highest calling. You've been the greatest role model and teacher. I only hope someday I can be as good you!

From Marti...

I too grew up in Ohio. Salineville, Ohio (population 1,397) is a little town that obviously had something good in the water—it produced me and Ben Feldman, the legendary life insurance salesman who sold more than a billion dollars' worth of life insurance during his career. He was so good at what he did that when his company, New York Life, ran a nationwide sales contest, he won by writing $15 million of new business in a month—at the age of 80.

In small towns, people understand that relationships count. The time spent on the front porch getting to know someone pays big dividends, not only for the initial sale, but for life. There are many lessons: loyalty comes from trust; trust comes from good listening; good listening comes from genuine caring.

And here's a tip for sales managers: you just might want to recruit in Salineville. I can tell you people understand loyalty, trust, good listening and genuine caring—foundations for a salesperson. Thanks, Ben Feldman. Thanks, Salineville.

From Marti and Rebecca...

To all of the amazing sales professionals in our lives—men and women, personal friends and clients—we offer a hearty "here's to you!". You've chosen a great profession. Thanks for generously sharing your stories so we could learn from and with you. We applaud your passion for selling, your tenacity to keep selling, and your willingness to try new approaches to make women your best, most loyal clients.

To our writer extraordinaire, Barry Schwenkmeyer, our heartfelt thanks for helping us find the right "voice". Your words, wisdom and wit are sure to inspire our readers.

To our extraordinary staff at Maddox Smye—you are simply the best. We couldn't have done it without your remarkable ability to support us and cheer us on at the same time.

To our loyal clients—who over the years have trusted us to teach and guide your sales people in new ways of relating and selling to their female clients. We celebrate your successes!

To our readers—writing this book has been a great adventure. The concepts and tools have been proven over and over in countless organizations across the United States and Canada. We only hope you will embrace the concepts and apply the tools. As always, we're solidly on your side! We promise you'll produce spectacular results.

INTRODUCTION

First, We're on YOUR Side

We need to say right up front that we are biased. We are unabashedly on your side—the side of the salesperson. We know that for you to grow sales, you will have to win the hearts, minds, and pocket-books of women.

This is not another book on marketing to women or teaching women to become better-educated consumers. Unfortunately, in spite of all the snazzy ads, beautiful brochures, and slick media spots aimed at females, women are not always buying. They're shopping and leaving—taking their money with them.

This book is about selling. It's about actually closing sales to women clients—effectively, time after time. Our research over the past 15 years verifies that selling to women is a science that can be learned. We encourage you to try it. We offer proven, practical methods and tools in each chapter.

Second, the Gender Issue

As you read this book you may be tempted to believe that it was written only for men. Actually, it is written for sale professionals—both men and women. You will receive equal benefit, but in slightly different ways.

Today's sales professionals, men and women, have been immersed in traditional male-oriented sales approaches. Female sales people have been required to adopt traditional sales methods in order to "fit in." And though times are changing, business cultures around the world are still predominantly male.

If you are a man reading this book, you will undoubtedly recognize some typical male responses to a woman's behavioral style. You'll gain important insights into a woman's way of thinking, connecting, listening, decision-making, and timing. And by using those insights to shape your behavior you'll see amazing results in your ability to sell effectively to women.

If you are a woman reading this book, you may additionally find that you deeply understand how and why women buyers respond as they do. And you may find you've learned a sales approach that is sabotaging your won innate ability to relate effectively with your female clients. You may need to unlearn old approaches as well as learn new tools and techniques.

Either way, we believe you'll see yourself and many of your clients in the following examples and stories. As a sales professional, man or women, we know that by practicing our approach, you will become RICH selling to women.

Now For Men ONLY

Now that we've said that...we do have one chapter "for men only." It's the last chapter, and it's for all you men who want to take the learning to the next level—not only to increase your sales to women, but to build richer relationships with all the wonderful women in your life.

Chapter 13 (yes, it's lucky!) will challenge you to translate your knowledge, skills, and techniques into a way of relating that will enhance your relationships for a lifetime. Enjoy the journey!

IT'S A WHOLE NEW BALL GAME

This book will show you how you can make more money than you have ever made before—by giving you the inside story on how to sell to a fast-growing and untapped market: women.

There are huge opportunities for selling to women out there, ripe for the plucking by anyone with the smarts to see them and the courage to try new ways of selling.

Thanks to the impact of the ever expanding women's movement, women have moved beyond fighting discrimination to demand equality. Today's woman has the power, the money, and the confidence to insist on buying products and services in the ways that work best for *her.* If you can't do business the way she wants, she'll find someone who can. No hard feelings. It's pretty much that simple.

The way most organizations are accustomed to selling is not in sync with the way most women want to buy.

Two converging trends have created this market.

Trend #1: Women are making more big-ticket purchases of traditionally male products

Women have moved beyond their traditional shopping venues. They now make big-ticket purchases of products and services—from building supplies to financial services to cars to electronics

INDUSTRIES WITH GROWING FEMALE CLIENT BASE

Financial Planning / Stocks and Bonds / Mortgages and Equity Loans / Banking Services / Cars / Boats / Motorcycles / New Houses / Building Supplies / Furniture / Computers / Broadband, Satellite, and Cable Systems / Security Systems / Heating and Cooling Systems

to heating and cooling systems—once bought almost exclusively by men.

At some point in the last five years, women became the major purchasers and/or purchase influencers of traditionally male-oriented products. Why? It's no mystery: women started earning more money. Although women's salaries still average less than men's, today 48% of working wives provide at least half of the family income.

You may already know that women make or control 80% of all consumer buying decisions. But here are some statistics that might surprise you:

- Women buy half of all sports equipment.
- Women accounted for over half of the $96 billion spent on electronics in 2003.[1]
- A third of all women consider themselves early adopters of cutting-edge technology.[2]
- More single women than single men buy houses.
- Women make up 48% of all investors in the stock market.[3]

Women's earnings have been increasing for some time. What's different now is that women have assets. Stocks and bonds. CD's. Rental property.

Trend #2: Women are embracing their D-gene

Remember when it was politically incorrect to imply that women and men were different in any but the most obvious

1 Study by the Consumer Electronics Association quoted in "Consumer Electronics Companies Woo Women," AP January 15, May Wong.

2 "Consumer Electronics Companies Woo Women"

3 Chapter 13: Women and Finance, from WOW statistics, Diversity *Best Practices/ Business Women's Network*, Washington DC

WOMEN-OWNED BUSINESSES[4]

Between 1997 and 2002 the number of women- and equally-owned businesses jumped by 11%, versus 6% among all privately-held businesses.

The fastest growth rates are in the traditionally male industries: construction, agricultural services, transportation, communications and public utilities.

Today there are over 10.1 million women- or equally-owned businesses. They employ 18.2 million people, and earn revenues of $2.32 trillion in sales.

ways? When women in business wore suits and blouses with those floppy little bow ties? When they would never wear a dress to work for fear that people might think they were—well, female?

In those days, when "different" often got translated to mean "inferior," there were perfectly good reasons to downplay these distinctions.

Today, women have reached a point where they can not only admit to but appreciate and insist on their differences from men. And the more they do, the more they respond to products, services and sales approaches that take these differences into account. In fact, so secure have women become about their differences from men that they can now laugh about them. Jokes about women get passed around the Internet—Did you hear about Buyagra? It's a stimulant taken prior to shopping that increases the duration and amount of spending. And it's often women who do the passing, and the laughing.

We refer to all male-female differences, both the biological and the culturally acquired, as the D-gene. The D-gene refers to differences in how men and women communicate, how they relate to other people, how they make decisions, how they evaluate situations and how they buy.

4 From National Women's Business Council, Fact Sheet July 2003

In Chapter 3, "Decoding the D-gene," we'll take a look at these differences. Although some are the product of social conditioning, you may be surprised to learn how many are genetic. Yes, now it can be told: men are hard-wired to be men, and women are hard-wired to be women.

The undecoded D-gene is often the reason some of life's charming little moments turn into great big ugly moments:

- a woman's willingness to ask directions versus a man's insistence on finding his own way
- a woman's interest in watching one TV show at a time versus a man's need to channel-surf
- a woman's interest in going shopping versus a man's interest in making a purchase

We all recognize these potential flash points, although we don't all leverage them as creatively as the woman who was making a purchase in a department store: as she reached into her purse for her wallet, the salesperson noticed a remote control device.

"Do you always carry your TV remote with you?" the salesperson asked.

"No," she replied, "but my husband refused to come shopping with me, so I figured this was the worst thing I could to do him without getting arrested."

What gives this little story that ring of truth that makes us laugh? The D-gene.

Please understand: we're not claiming that one gender is better than the other. It's the D (for different) gene, remember, not the B (for better) gene. And we're certainly not saying that men don't try to bridge the gap. It's just that if you haven't decoded the D-gene, the gap can be virtually unbridgeable.

Take the man who was attending a marriage seminar with his wife. At one point the leader said that a good husband will always know his wife's favorite flower. Hearing this, the husband smiled, leaned over to his wife, gently touched her arm, and whispered proudly, "It's Pillsbury, isn't it?"

This guy is obviously sincere. He thinks he "got it," so what's the problem? Why the disconnect?

Right. It's the damned D-gene.

Even if you "get it," can you "do it"? The purpose of this book is to help you improve your sales to women, not your personal relationships, although we have found that one leads to the other. (More about that later.) We bring up these lighter moments because they illustrate at a domestic level the problem we find in sales organizations throughout North America.

Here's the situation, and, given the hugely expanded role women play in today's society, it's a surprising one: by now, at the beginning of the twenty-first century, most organizations have made progress in reaching out to women—a little in some cases, a lot in others. Even organizations that sell traditionally male products have figured out how to make their marketing communications appeal to women. So, for example, we see an ad for long-term care insurance that shows two older women hiking in the woods and talking about preparing for the future.

Organizations are also making great strides in developing products designed with women in mind. One of the most exciting recent examples is Volvo's YCC (Your Concept Car), which was designed by and for women:

- The owner of a YCC will never have to lift the hood; in fact, you can't lift the hood. The car communicates with the dealership to check systems and schedule maintenance.
- Because women use the backseat for carrying packages more often than for passengers, the rear seats are folded up like theatre seats.
- Owners will be able to swap their seat covers and carpets whenever they want a new interior color scheme.

- There is even a function that determines if there is enough room in a parallel parking spot, and then helps steer the car into it.

It remains to be seen how many of these concept-car features make their way into Volvo's production models. What seems clear, however, is that we have come a long way from that 1955 lavender-and-pink Dodge with rosebud upholstery.

Given this progress, it is all the more remarkable that the way sales organizations sell to women has remained virtually unchanged, despite the changes of the last three decades. Companies still use pretty much the same spiel and the same techniques they did when most of their clients were men.

Whatever sensitivity about women's issues may exist in the executive suite or the marketing department doesn't always get to the sales force. This is puzzling, because in terms of client impact, selling is where the rubber hits the road. Nevertheless, few salespeople know the specifics of how women like to go about making a purchase. Of those who do, fewer still can translate their awareness into effective female-focused selling behaviors.

Nowhere does an organization reveal its attitude towards women more vividly than in the behavior of its sales force.

There is a huge gulf between what we know we *should* do and our ability to actually do it, especially when the stakes are high. Take a look at any sport, and you'll see what we mean. Every golfer in the world knows you're supposed to keep your head down when you make a shot, right? So why don't they always do it?

Behavioral change isn't easy, and it doesn't happen overnight, especially when it involves something as ingrained as how we deal with the world as men, or as women. It's one thing for a company to "celebrate women," and put out female-focused marketing materials. It's another thing for a sales force to learn female-friendly selling behaviors thoroughly enough to use them consistently and effectively with women.

When we learn a new behavior, there is usually an old behavior we have to "unlearn." It takes courage to set aside old ways to try new approaches, especially when these old ways worked for us in the past. It also takes a willingness to practice these new approaches, and a realization that to reach new levels of success you may have to go through a period of feeling a little awkward.

We are here to tell you that your opportunities for success with this new market are more than worth the effort. We believe that traditional male-oriented selling practices are the major stumbling block in an organization's attempt to engage successfully with women clients. Update your selling practices, and the sky becomes the limit.

WHAT THIS BOOK CAN DO FOR YOU

So here's the deal: the people who will get women's business will be those who take the trouble to decode the D-gene in the context of the product or service they sell, and adapt their behaviors accordingly. Using the concepts in this book, you will be able to create sales experiences for your women clients that are uniquely tailored to their needs and preferences.

We will give you these insights into successfully selling to women:

MORE THAN / LESS THAN

When you sell to women, you do some things the same and some things differently. Mostly you do things "more than" or "less than" you would with your male clients.

- What women want at every point in a sales relationship
- What turns women off—immediately, and over time
- When to pursue, and when to back off
- How to encourage women to communicate their concerns directly to you
- How to read the subtle cues (surprisingly different from men's) that let you know how women are responding

Selling successfully to women does not require you to set aside everything you have ever learned about selling. You'll be able to stay within the guidelines of your existing selling process—although as you become more effective, you may find yourself using these concepts with all your clients, men as well as women.

Decoding the D-gene will pay off in several ways:

- bigger and more sales to women
- greater likelihood of successful cross-selling
- a higher conversion rate for your female prospects
- a growing group of loyal women clients—the kind who not only stick with you but also tell their friends about you
- more success with your male clients and prospects and finally...
- an improvement in your relationships with the women in your life

Is this book for you? Check out the following chart and see for yourself:

Do you...	Then this book will...
1. Consider yourself already successfully selling to women?	Help you build on your success with some new tips and techniques.
2. Strive to treat male and female clients basically the same?	Increase your rate of success by showing you exactly how and under which circumstances women appreciate being treated differently.
3. Deal with your female clients by trying to be "softer" and avoiding statistics?	Demonstrate steps that create the difference between so-so results and get-rich success.

Do you...	Then this book will...
4. See women clients as mysteries; you never know where you stand with them, and are happy simply to avoid being offensive?	Give you the confidence to create successful sales strategies specifically designed with your women clients in mind.
5. Think most women suffer from male gender envy?	Challenge your thinking—enough, perhaps, to blast you out of your cave and into some successful sales to women.
6. Think of women as the less intelligent half of the world and speak down to them?	Expand your thinking and help you realize different is not dumb.

And remember, if you're a female sales professional, this book will give you permission to tap into your D-gene, and use it to make strong and profitable connections with your women clients.

A FINAL WORD

Throughout these pages you may take issue with some statements about the differences between men and women. "Wait a minute!" you might say. "I know plenty of women who don't behave—or think or feel—that way, and plenty of men who do!"

We do too. We recognize that all of us live on a continuum of human behavior with many areas of overlap and very few hard-and-fast divisions. Not all women like to shop, for example, just as not all men refuse to ask for directions. However, as general statements these differences describe most men and women, and we stand by them.

In the final analysis, of course, an effective sales associate needs to go beyond generalities to respond to each client as a unique individual with a unique set of needs.

We believe that the insights and advice we offer here will help you do just that...—move beyond the barriers of gender differences to establish profitable, long-term relationships with your female clients, client by client.

2 THE WOMEN'S MARKET FOR INSURANCE AND ANNUITIES

Here's a question:

Why is it that the average value of life insurance policies purchased by men is twice that of policies purchased by women?

It can't be because women rely on their husbands for support. Women are more independent and self-reliant than ever before—perhaps because they know that over one million marriages end in divorce each year. Here are the facts:

- Over 9 million U. S. businesses, 40% of the total, are owned by women. These businesses are not loving, hands-at-home operations. They produce over $3.6 trillion in annual revenue, and create one in every four jobs.
- In 2002, 19.4 million single women owned their own homes.[1]
- Thirty-one percent of all married working women earn more than their husbands.[2] Forty-eight percent provide at least half of their household's incomes.
- Women head 40% of households with assets of over $600,000.

1 Census Bureau's Marital Status and Living Arrangements: 2002

2 Bureau of Labor Statistics, cited by Rebecca in her 4/12/05 interview. (1999 LIMRA study says "over 20%," as quoted in "It's Time to Turn the Potential of the Women's Market into Real Sales," in Nat'l Underwriter, 1/13/2003.)

➤ Today's women are postponing marriage. At the same time, more and more single women are choosing to have babies—with the greatest increase among white, college-educated women.[3]

Nor can it be because women can't afford insurance. Women's financial profiles become more impressive with each passing year:

> *"Given the large gains that women have made in the labor force and the fact that one in five wives earn more than her husband, agents are overlooking wives, especially at the high-income levels."*
>
> *Nilufer R. Ahmed, Ph.D.* The Women's Market: Myth and Reality, *LIMRA International, 1999*

➤ According to the 2000 U.S. Census, three million women earned more than $75,000 a year—and 1.3 million of them earned more than $100,000.[4]

➤ Women are closing the earnings gap. Although women of all ages earn only 73 cents for every dollar earned by men, that figure for younger women now entering the workforce is 83 cents.[5]

➤ Affluent women are younger than their male counterparts, which means that more of them are still working—and therefore have more time to increase their net worth.[6] Women are projected to have 50% of U.S. private wealth by 2010. That's roughly $12.5 trillion. With a T.[7]

➤ Women represent 52% of the U.S. population over age 18.[8]

And it certainly isn't that women are not interested in insurance. As you'll see in Chapter 3, women have a genetic affinity for the security that insurance products bring.

The real answer may be that while insurance companies today may *market* to women, the people who do the actual *selling*—the

3 "High Potential, Yet Underserved…"

4 Advising Affluent Women," by Nilufer Ahmed, LIMRA International

5 "High Potential, Yet Underserved…"

6 A Business Proposal: High Net Worth Women: Capturing the Market

7 Conde Nast Publications

8 U.S. Census Data 2002, Release Date June/2003

insurance agents, brokers, producers, financial services providers, advocates, or insurance sales professionals—may not yet have decided that the women's market is worth going after.

We are here to tell you that it is worth going after.

To start with, there is a natural fit between women and insurance.

- Women's concern with guaranteeing a secure future for themselves and their loved ones makes them natural clients for ***life insurance.*** Statistics indicate, however, that the focus of sales remains on the husband, and the financial burdens on the family his death would create. Yet today, chances are the death of a wife will also mean a substantial loss in income for the family. Plus, who's the husband going to get to cook, clean, take care of the kids, and everything else his wife did at home?
- Or take ***long-term care insurance.*** Because a woman knows relatives will look to her for the care of an aging and ailing spouse or parent, she can understand better than anyone else the value of long-term care insurance. Although women have traditionally been the caregivers, today a woman can't afford to walk away from her career to stay home and care for parents or a husband, nor does she necessarily want to. And when she grows old and frail, she doesn't want to depend on her grown children, either.
- What this means is that, even though she may have other investments, a woman is likely to be interested in anything— like an ***annuity***—that will provide her a guaranteed income for as long as she lives.

Perhaps a woman's greatest fear is losing her independence in old age. Most women, in fact, fear that they will outlive their assets. This is not unreasonable. Although the gap is narrowing, women live on average of six years longer than men. Did you know that the average age of a new widow is 56? That's right: 56.

> "Women have a great fear of being a bag lady, no matter what their income," according to Karen Minyard, managing director of Women's Financial Services Network at PNC Advisors. In an article in *Bank Investment Marketing,* she put it this way: "[Women] know the statistics. They know they make less money than men do. They are in and out of the workforce. They live longer. They take care of all the health care in their family, so they're acutely aware of how expensive that is. So they worry more."[9]

WHAT'S GOING ON?

For all these reasons, you would think that the insurance industry would be all over the women's market—if for no other reason than that there is less competition selling to a woman than to a man.

The industry has made strides with women. In 1984, to take just one example, insured women owned just 42% of the individual life coverage owned by insured men. This translates into women owning less than 30% of the entire individual life coverage. By 1998 this proportion had grown to 54%. Nevertheless, tremendous opportunities and untapped potentials are out there, and the question is, "Why?"

Two reasons.

First, although many insurance companies have gone to some lengths to reach out to women, the fact is that the insurance industry is still pretty much male-oriented. Although the executive team and the corporate folks in Marketing may "get" the women's market, the companies have done little if anything to adapt the way they sell to the way women want to buy. Please understand that we are not casting blame in any direc-

9 "What Women Really Want," by Karen Krebsbach, *Bank Investment Marketing,* May 2001.

tion. We recognize that over the years the insurance industry has developed innovative products that have helped men and women at all income levels to protect and grow their assets, so that they can provide a secure future for themselves and their families.

The second reason is that many insurance products have become a commodity—bought on price—and as a result most of us no longer have much of a relationship with an insurance agent. Instead, we use the phone. We get quotes on the Internet. We enroll at work. We end up with a bunch of different policies—car, health, homeowner's, liability, life, etc.—but no sense of our overall insurance picture. Are we sufficiently well covered? Are we paying too much? Who knows? There doesn't seem to be anyone whose job it is to help us figure it out.

IT'S THE RELATIONSHIP

In the rest of this book we're going to tell you everything you need to know about how to sell life and long-term care insurance, as well as annuities, to women. But here's a headline: it all boils down to relationships. If you want to sell successfully to women, you need to know how to develop and maintain thoughtful, creative, honest, and proactive long-term relationships with your female clients.

Having a trusting relationship with you is more important to a woman client than knowing your performance record.

Yes, we know—everyone tries to develop relationships with his or her clients. The relationships we're talking about, however, are different from the kinds of relationships you may have with male clients: these are a little deeper, a little more "human," and a lot less cut-and-dried. They call for a new understanding and new behaviors. You'll probably need to pay a little more attention, be a little more creative, and share a lot more of yourself than you

A BIG CHALLENGE FOR INSURANCE SALES PROFESSIONALS

Establishing a relationship with clients when the products they sell are becoming commodities.

are used to. And we don't mean in a canned speech about the facts of your life ("Well, I'm married with two children, and I've been here 14 years, and..."), but in smaller moments that enable you to establish common ground and let her know the kind of a person you are ("I know what you mean. If a restaurant is too noisy, I don't care how good the food is").

THE POWER OF THE PAST

Before we go any further, there are a few things that need to be said about how women regard financial services in general. You probably won't hear them from your women clients, but if you want to be successful selling to women, these are things you need to know.

As we said, most women still assume that insurance, like other parts of the financial services industry, is male-oriented, with male professional employees and male clients, and a corresponding masculine slant to its business practices. Therefore, before we tell you how you can adapt these selling practices to the way women like to buy, we need to talk about the power of this assumption, because it still exerts a strong influence on a woman's expectations and concerns when she thinks about doing business with you.

When a woman works with an insurance agent, she probably feels, at a level that may not be conscious, that she's playing a man's game. This is true even though:

- she may in more familiar areas be confident and have the ability to assert her needs.
- she may be wealthy and financially sophisticated, as more and more women are today.
- she may have a high-powered job.

➤ she may manage her own business and/or family finances.

➤ she may even be working with a woman agent.

In the back of her mind there still lurks the feeling that she's operating in foreign territory. She may not even be aware of this feeling until something happens to trigger it.

Many wives experience this awareness when they're sitting around the kitchen table with their husbands, discussing life insurance with an insurance agent. Ironically, the agent may be sitting there only because the wife decided the family was underinsured.In other words, at that moment she is the agent's biggest friend, his strongest ally.

So what does the agent do? He gives the couple some brochures, making sure the wife sees the special women's programs his company supports. Soon, however, he's trading sports statistics with the husband, and then telling him about various insurance options that he assumes the wife either can't understand or won't be interested in. (How much the husband actually understands is another story.) Later on, when the couple doesn't return his calls, he wonders why he didn't get their business.

If you're a man, you may have a hard time imagining how alienated and powerless this treatment can make a woman feel. If you've ever made a purchase in the lingerie department, you may have felt awkward and a little silly—but that's different from feeling patronized and excluded.

To be successful with women, it's not enough to be good at your job. You also have to be good as a person. This means being honest, having integrity, and consistently doing the right thing.

Women have antennae that unfailingly pick up all kinds of details, and will spot the slightest indication of condescension or patronizing behavior a mile away—even if you didn't intend it. They can tell—as this wife could—when the details don't add up. Thought the agent's company may showcase its "female focus," its true nature emerges in its face-to-face interactions.

Because a man might not take such treatment personally, you may find a woman's reaction hard to understand. Perhaps you think the woman is being overly-sensitive; but if you want to succeed as a sales professional, you need to do everything in your power to avoid sending signals indicating you're giving her anything less than your total respect and attention.

WHAT YOUR WOMEN CLIENTS AREN'T TELLING YOU

If one of your women clients feels she is being discounted and tells you about it, consider yourself lucky. At least you know what the problem is, and stand a fighting chance of fixing it. More often, women who feel themselves treated badly will say nothing, find a graceful way to leave, and never come back. Why? Because they don't have the time to get into it, they don't like to be confrontational, or they figure that no matter what they say, you're a lost cause. But guess what? Even if they don't tell you, they'll tell twenty of their friends. That's the power of female networking, and we'll tell you how you can put it to positive use later in the book.

But what about the women who stay and say nothing? That must mean they're happy, right? Well, here are a couple of recent findings about financial services that shed new light on supposedly satisfied women clients:

- Women say insurance products are too hard to understand.
- 84% of women in a Yankelovich survey said they felt misunderstood by investment professionals.[10]
- 55% of affluent women feel they are not taken as seriously by their financial advisers as men are.[11]

10 Brand Notes (newsletter), Vol. 1, Issue 110, May 2003

11 She Said. Study conducted by Maddox Smye, Deloitte, Yankelovich Partners, 1998.

Although they shared these feelings with a researcher, they didn't share them with their financial professionals.

Why? Women are more relationship-oriented than men, and because of their cultural conditioning they are less likely than men to rock the boat. Women are very experienced at adapting themselves to men; older women, especially, may not realize there's any other way—even in situations where they are the clients. The question is: how loyal are such women in these situations? Do you think they would stay with their insurance representatives through thick and thin? Don't bet on it—not if a D-gene-savvy sales representative came along.

We know of a woman in her middle 50's who had been working with an insurance agent for years. "Every two years he'd come over and talk about the cost of living and the need for increased coverage, blah blah blah. He'd ask how I was and what had happened since the last time we spoke, but I could tell he was just waiting to jump in and make his recommendation. Then a friend told me that she had an agent who was a really good listener, and who really understood her situation and what she needed. He's my agent now."

ALL THE MORE REASON FOR DEVELOPING A STRONG RELATIONSHIP

These are the top reasons men and women give (right after "too expensive") for not buying life insurance:

- *Could not decide on policy type or coverage amount (37%)*
- *Afraid of making the wrong decision (26%)*
- *Did not know enough about life insurance (23%)*

(If these percentages are true for both men and women, do you think they might just possibly be higher for women?)

As you'll see in the next chapter, a woman wants to feel confident she can rely on her broker or financial adviser to do whatever is necessary to make her experience a positive one. This explains why, when asked to describe positive experiences with a financial services provider, women mentioned examples of service six times more frequently than examples of financial performance or success.[12]

12 She Said

So what *don't* women like about their agents, brokers, and financial advisers? Here's a list of quotes from some interviews we conducted with women clients concerning people who sold all kinds of financial products. As an insurance agent or broker, do you recognize yourself in any of these comments?

- *He doesn't listen.* "I can tell the minute his attention wanders. You know, I get enough glazed-eye listening from my husband at the dinner table. From my agent I expect better."
- *He monopolizes the conversation.* "Even the ones who ask questions can't seem to stop talking long enough for me to answer."
- *He assumes my husband has the final word.* "Our agent would call and pitch a product or policy to me. When I agreed to buy, he'd say, 'Is this something you and your husband both want?' We don't get any more of these insulting calls, because we moved our account."
- *She's not warm or outgoing.* "The atmosphere in my bank is so chilly. Do they all hate their jobs? I would never buy insurance from them."
- *He doesn't return my calls.* "When I had an insurance question, I could never get anyone on the phone to answer it. Now I work with an agent who has given me her home phone number."
- *She rushes me.* "I always get the impression that if I don't act right away, I'll lose out. I can't make decisions under that kind of pressure.In fact, I think it's my agent who's worried about losing out…on a quick commission."
- *He brags.* "I'm not saying he's lying; I know he's good. But whenever he starts tooting his own horn, I turn off. Is he so insecure that he thinks he needs to do that?"

WHAT DO AGENTS AND FINANCIAL SERVICES SALESPERSONS SAY ABOUT THE CHALLENGES OF WORKING WITH WOMEN CLIENTS?

If that's what women have to say about people who sell financial services products, what do these sales professionals have to say about their women clients? Here are some typical comments:

- *I never know where I stand with them.* "If I make a presentation to a guy, and he doesn't buy, I figure, 'Oh well, win some, lose some.' With a woman, I always wonder, 'Did I do something wrong? Did I offend her in some way?'"
- *They pay more attention to their hairdressers than they do to me.* "I've got a client with a whole network of 'advisers.' I make a recommendation, and the next week she asks six different people about it, and of course she gets six different opinions. My advice doesn't seem to count for any more than her unemployed brother-in-law's."
- *They tell me their life stories.* "I mean, OK, their grandson is cute. But then they tell me about their son and his wife and their problems, and on and on and on. I really am willing to listen. The problem is, I've scheduled an hour for our meeting, and by the end of the hour nothing has happened."
- *They ask too many questions.* "Women can get so intense. The more I tell them, the more they ask me. It's like they're trying to cover any possible eventuality. Some of that's a good thing, but lighten up, is what I say."
- *They take too long to make decisions.* "I'll call her—you know, check in to see where she is. But I get the feeling she doesn't want to be pressured, so now I don't know how to move things along. We could both be dead before she decides."

THE IRONY OF THE SITUATION

If you look at what the salespeople say, it's all about women not fitting into the traditional way the salespeople are used to doing business. Women take too long, talk too much, and ask too many questions.

WOMEN ARE INCLINED TO INVEST

- *93% of women fear not having enough money in their old age.*
- *77% want financial independence*
- *72% choose conservatively, low risk and return*

Prudential Securities Women Cents Survey

Women's complaints, on the other hand, center around the lack of a personal relationship. Agents don't listen. They're not friendly. They treat clients impersonally. They don't return calls.

The irony is that, despite all the salespeople's complaints, research demonstrates that women are more disposed than men to listen to people they perceive as trustworthy experts:

- Women are more likely to rely on a trusted person for financial advice. Men are twice as likely to rely on newspapers, newsletters, and magazines.[13]
- 90% of women look to their financial advisers to teach as well as advise them. Only 75% of men feel this way.[14]
- Women are more loyal than men. Once a woman feels she can trust you, she'll stay with you. A man, on the other hand, is more focused on the deal. If he can get a better deal elsewhere, he's likely to move on.

If, as an insurance agent, you want to tap into the enormous women's market, the message is clear: you need to spend at least as much time establishing trusting relationships with your women clients as you do developing your product savvy and technical expertise. The secret lies in your ability to adapt what you do to the needs

Products and services eventually become commodities. The only lasting competitive advantage lies in human interaction.

13 *Time,* May 22, 2002

14 Oppenheimer Funds Survey

and preferences of your women clients throughout a sale: from the critical initial minutes of a first meeting to the sale's close; from service and support after the sale to maintaining an ongoing relationship with your client that will produce additional leads and sales in the future.

And how do you do this? The first step is learning how to decode the D-gene. That's the topic of the next chapter.

3 DECODING THE D-GENE

What are the differences between men and women—and why should you care about them? So far we've been talking about the D-gene in general terms. Now it's time to get specific.

> **BLAME IT ON THE D-GENE #1**
>
> *A* **woman** *worries about the future until she gets a husband.*
>
> *A* **man** *never worries about the future until he gets a wife.*

In this chapter we will concentrate on the four areas of male-female differences that have the greatest impact on the buying (and therefore the selling) process:

- How men and women relate to other people
- How they express themselves
- How they take in and process information
- How they make decisions

This is the information you need to maximize your sales to women. It can mean the difference between striking out (or making a one-time sale) and creating loyal clients who trust you to do what's best for them over the long haul.

WHERE DO THE DIFFERENCES COME FROM?

Are women different from men because of their genetic make-up or because of how they were raised? There's no simple answer to this nature-nurture debate, although recent research seems to be swinging the pendulum towards nature. In other words, you can forbid your young son to play with toy guns, but don't be surprised if he chews a piece of toast into the shape of a pistol and starts firing away.

BLAME IT ON THE D-GENE #2

Why do women always have the last word?

Because anything a man says after that becomes the beginning of the next argument.

We are all products of our evolution. The male-female differences that developed many thousands of years ago to insure the perpetuation of our species live on in each of us, even though we no longer need them to survive and they no longer limit the roles we play. Everyone knows that women today can be bread-winners, and men can stay home and raise children. Etc.

Nevertheless, some significant male-female differences remain, stronger in some individuals than in others. They are at the root of the tension between the sexes that people often defuse through humor (see the "Blame it on the D-gene" boxes in this chapter). When it comes to selling successfully to women, however, these differences deliver more than a few laughs. Once you understand them, you have the keys to the kingdom.

Our purpose here is to help you increase your sales. It would be a mistake at this point to veer off into an argument over which differences are better. There is no better or worse, there is only different. The only point we want to make is that a sales professional can use this understanding to accommodate him or herself to the preferences of women clients; and as a result achieve greater success in terms of initial sales, loyal clients, repeat business, and referrals.

Any discussion of the D-gene has got to start with *hormones* (don't worry—this is not a biology lecture). Most people know that testosterone is the male hormone, and estrogen the primary female hormone, although women have some testosterone, and men have some estrogen.

- *Testosterone* is what makes men strong, competitive, aggressive, and inclined to take risks. Research tells us that testosterone also contributes to such other traits as math and analytical ability, mechanical skills, and a talent for navigating and reading maps. (There is no indication that it facilitates operation of a television remote control.) These qualities were vital in the days when men had to compete for and keep mates, hunt for food, and protect their families against danger.

- *Estrogen* is the female equivalent of testosterone. It increases a woman's interest in nest-building and nurturing. Another hormone, *progesterone,* triggers the maternal feelings she needs to bond with her infant. *Oxytocin,* which helps induce labor, also facilitates mother-and-child bonding. In fact, during some moments of stress, when men release the adrenaline that produces the "fight or flight" syndrome, women release oxytocin, which drives them to seek safety and solace with others, a response that is sometimes referred to as "tend and befriend." In fact, researchers now believe oxytocin helps women form healthy interpersonal relationships of all kinds.

RELATIONSHIP-ORIENTED FROM THE GET-GO

Female infants sustain eye contact twice as long as boys. They're also better at distinguishing between photos of people they know and people they don't.

- Researchers also believe that women's higher levels of the hormone *seratonin* reduce their aggression and interest in risk-taking activities.

A woman's interest in forming emotional connections with other people is permanent and deep-seated. This is why it's so important to establish a trustworthy relationship with your woman clients, and why they are not motivated by the competition that drives many sales to men.

THE FEMALE BRAIN

A woman's brain is indeed wired differently from a man's. Men's brains tend to have clearly separated functions. Women's brains, by and large, tend to have more internal connections, within and across hemispheres. Women's emotional centers, for example, are found in many parts of the brain, while men's are concentrated in the right side. This interconnected distribution may support a broader, more nonlinear thinking style in women, in contrast to a man's more focused approach.

> **BLAME IT ON THE D-GENE #3**
>
> *A successful* **man** *is one who makes more money than his wife can spend.*
>
> *A successful* **woman** *is one who can find such a man.*

This difference is good to keep in mind while you listen to a woman tell you what her financial needs are. Instead of trying to control your impatience with her rambling, if you can instead tune into her different style of thinking, you'll find you can listen attentively and with respect. The payoff for you—you'll gain valuable information—and you'll earn her loyalty.

EXPECTATIONS OF SOCIETY

Although the gap between the rules for males and females has certainly narrowed in the last forty years, there is still plenty of social pressure on women and girls to be quiet, compliant, and "polite," and not to get angry or interrupt others.

As a sales professional, therefore, you need to make sure you don't unwittingly play into these pressures by making her "fight" to get her point across. You need to avoid assuming that her compliance equals agreement and encourage (but not pressure) her to speak up.

THE D-GENE AND SELLING TO WOMEN

With this quick background, let's return to the four sales-related areas where the D-gene has the biggest impact, and take a look at what you can do to accommodate your sales approach to how women like to buy.

As you read, think about your current sales process. Is the way you sell a male-oriented approach? Is it tailored primarily to men? Do you see places where you can modify your approach to respond to women's preferences?

Again, keep in mind that we are talking about *most* men and *most* women. Don't get hung up on the people you may know who behave differently. Once you get the overall model, you can modify your approach to fit people who exhibit a combination of male and female characteristics.

1. How men and women relate to other people

Men see themselves as independent operators who relate to others by achieving goals and solving problems; there is often a strong element of competition involved. Women see themselves in terms of their relationships, and relate to others by sharing and establishing emotional connections. For example:

Women	Men
Woman are relationship-oriented. They derive identity from their place in relationships.	Men are transaction-oriented; they derive identity from what they do and achieve.
Women are conditioned to get along, be nice. They work to ensure win/win outcomes. They like to share, equalize, work together. They see themselves as part of a culture of equals.	Men are raised on and comfortable with competition and win/lose outcomes. A man sees himself as part of a hierarchy, with some people above and some below him. Men are more comfortable in a command-and-control environment.

Women	Men
Women thrive on courtesy and respect. Politeness and manners, insofar as they build bridges and avoid conflict, mean a lot to them. The closer competition gets to overt conflict, the more uncomfortable women become with it.	Men thrive on competition. They see negotiation as a challenging game in which they can test their skills and perhaps dominate the other person. Their physical contact with other men is often rough and jostling.
A woman's style is to create community, brainstorm with others, build consensus.	A man's style is to dominate, interrupt, give advice, and do more telling than asking.
Women tend to be open to the input and influence of others.	Men resist being influenced by others; they prefer to be seen as making up their own minds.

SELLING TIPS

Whatever you can do to establish and maintain a relationship with a woman client will make her feel more comfortable, and therefore more likely to buy from you. Establishing such a connection should be your primary goal; if you do that, the sale will almost take care of itself.

> **BLAME IT ON THE D-GENE #4**
>
> **Men at lunch:** *When a bill for $52.50 arrives, each of the four guys will throw in a twenty. None will have anything smaller— and no one will admit to wanting any change back.*
>
> **Women at lunch:** *When the bill arrives, out come the pocket calculators.*

- One way to build a relationship is to find commonalities in your lives—children, hobbies, favorite authors, travel—and share them. Remember to ask about them whenever you talk.
- Look for times when you can share your feelings. That's right: feelings. Let's face it—you'll never create a strong personal bond by discussing the ins and outs of a 401(k) plan. The more you open up, the more she'll trust you. Don't be afraid to ask about her thoughts and feelings, either.

- Introduce her to "your team," the people you work with who may be involved in servicing her account at some point. Let her know that these people are also "her team," and that they are very important to you.
- Host gatherings that bring together your women clients and/or prospects. Make sure these events are small enough for people to get to know each other.

2. *How men and women express themselves*

This just in: women talk more than men. In one study women clocked in at 25,000 words a day (versus 12,000 for men). As a man, you may think women talk primarily to transmit information. Wrong. That's what *men* do. Women also talk to connect, to check on and maintain relationships, to find their place in a group, and to feel safe. For example:

Women	Men
Women like communication with more context, emotional content, and detail. They tend to tell the whole story, starting at the beginning.	Men like communication that is concise, streamlined, and often focused on specific actions or results.
Women value communication as a way to interact, express emotions and offer intuitions.	Men value communication as a way to give and receive information, discover and express facts.
Women talk more often in terms of preferences and suggestions. They ask more question than men.	Men talk more often in terms of information and advice. They ask fewer questions.

Women	Men
Women's language is characterized by disclaimers ("I'm no expert, but...") and qualifiers ("Don't you think we should..."). They make fewer direct statements than men.	Men's language is more direct, with fewer qualifiers than women. It's also characterized by teasing, joking, and verbal bantering.
Women tend to disclose personal information about themselves as part of establishing connections with others.	Men tend not to disclose personal information. It's their way of protecting their independence, and keeping their options open.
Women make eye contact while talking with another person.	Men make less eye contact while talking with others.
Women interrupt less. They also allow more interruptions, although they don't like being interrupted.	Men interrupt more, and allow fewer interruptions.

SELLING TIPS

- Don't waste your time trying to cut a woman off, or hurry her story along. She won't like it, and besides, you can't do it. The fact is, if you know how to listen, everything a woman says is golden. If you pay attention to what she says, you'll eventually be able to offer products and services that fit perfectly into her life, including some she may not even know she needs.
- Don't assume that just because she doesn't always cut to the chase, she doesn't know what she wants. A woman may soften assertions with various qualifiers: "That's awfully expensive, isn't it?" but don't assume she's not serious or well-informed.
- Maintain eye contact. If you're a man, this might feel awkward at first; when men talk, they tend not to look

at each other as much as women do. To a woman, not looking her in the eye makes you seem shifty and untrustworthy.

- Don't interrupt. Or, to put it another way: DON'T INTERRUPT! For men, interrupting and being interrupted is part of the normal give-and-take of a conversation. The better the conversation, the more the interruptions. Not so for a woman. Women wait their turn. Nothing makes a woman feel more irritated or discounted than being interrupted. You may know where her conversation is heading. You may know exactly what she needs. You may have an exciting idea you just can't wait to present. Forget about it. Bite your tongue until it's bloody, if you need to, but...don't interrupt.

BLAME IT ON THE D-GENE #5

"Of course we talk more than men," one woman said. "We have to say everything twice because men don't listen."

3. *How men and women take in and process information*

Think of a funnel with information going in the top and coming out the bottom. With a woman, the funnel stays wider longer and takes in a greater variety of information. With a man, it narrows sooner, discarding extraneous data along the way. For example:

Women	Men
Women see themselves as students. They're comfortable asking for help and admitting what they don't know.	Men see themselves as masters of a situation. They're less comfortable asking for help and admitting what they don't know.

Women	Men
Women think more concretely, often organizing information into stories.	Men think more abstractly. They look for principles, rules, patterns.
When applying the rules, women are often more interested in the person's circumstances than in an abstract notion of good and bad. They use their own experiences and examples to make decisions.	Men often see situations in abstract terms of right and wrong, good and bad. They are more likely than women to think that the rules should be applied equally to everyone.
Women listen actively and physically —nodding, smiling, gesturing.	Men listen passively. Often they show little or no response at all.
Women nod to indicate they are listening.	Men nod to indicate agreement.
Women are more sensitive than men to body language, emotional states, and nonverbal cues.	Men tend to focus on the objective facts.
Women seek to expand their perspective and search out options.	Men tend to analyze, sifting through facts to eliminate those that don't apply so they can zero in on the key points.

SELLING TIPS

- Do less lecturing. With women disposed to listen and ask questions, and men disposed to see themselves as experts, the temptation to pontificate can be powerful. Resist it at all costs.
- Tell more stories when you talk about your products. Include your client in them—her goals, her needs, her family, her future.
- LISTEN. This, of course, is the flip side of NO INTERRUPTING.
- *Show* that you're listening. Nod, say "mm hmm," and inject a response from time to time to let her know you're track-

ing. Remember, a woman can usually spot someone who is only pretending to listen.

4. How men and women make buying decisions

For a woman, making a purchase in a traditionally male industry will almost always be a high-stakes decision, regardless of the cost of the product. Along with her lack of experience in the area, and a concern that she may be taken advantage of, she does not want to get home and have her husband or boyfriend say, "They really sold you a bill of goods! How much did you pay¿!" For example:

Women	Men
Women feel a need to make the "perfect" or "right" decision.	Men are generally satisfied with a "good" decision.
Women tend to buy a relationship. They are influenced by how they're treated.	Men tend to buy a product. They are influenced by the deal they got.
A woman often begins the buying process by talking with others she knows who are knowledgeable.	Men tend to begin the process with independent research.
A woman's buying process encompasses a circular search pattern, involving thinking, discussing, comparing, and collaborating. For her, a purchase is about the process.	A man's buying process is more linear—from research to the purchase. For him, it's about solving a problem.
Women express interest in what a product or service does for them and for those who matter to them.	Men express interest in a product's or service's efficiencies, and how it works.
Women take longer to decide, but in the end are more loyal clients.	Men make quicker decisions, but are fickle and less loyal.

BLAME IT ON THE D-GENE #6

A woman asks her husband to help her shop for a dress for an upcoming cocktail party. "I was thinking of something red," she says.

As soon as they get to the store, he spots a red dress on the rack and says, "This looks nice. Why don't you try it on?"

When she comes out of the dressing room, she looks really great and he tells her so.

She agrees— which is why he's surprised when she insists they check out what other stores have to offer.

And at the end of the day, which dress does she buy? Right, the one they saw first.

What the husband thinks they did: waste their time.

What the wife thinks they did: research.

SELLING TIPS

- Be patient. Don't indicate in any way that she's taking too long to make up her mind. (And don't forget that women are experts at reading body language.)
- Prepare yourself for second (and third and fourth) opinions. A woman may seek advice from everyone she knows; and when it comes to life insurance or annuities, for example, you can be sure they will each have their two cents to add. You may be irritated at having your advice equated with your client's hairdresser's, but there isn't much you can do about it.
- Keep the relationship uppermost in your mind, because she certainly will. You may have put together a first-class analysis of her insurance needs, but if you don't return her calls promptly, she may not return yours—ever.
- Help her connect emotionally with the product by showing how it will make her life better, as well as the lives of those she cares about.

Now that you know about the D-gene and what it is telling you, you're ready to apply your new knowledge to the fine-tuning of your overall selling approach.

4 NOT UNTIL SHE TRUSTS YOU

What Women Want Most in a Buying Experience

Research tells us that when it comes to making large purchases, men look first for value, the deal they're able to get; next comes the salesperson's likeability; and finally the salesperson's trustworthiness.

"I felt manipulated towards a choice which had nothing to do with what I needed. I couldn't see how it would benefit me in any way."

With women, it's exactly the opposite. Before anything else, a woman needs to trust the sales professional she's working with, especially in a traditional male industry. Then comes likeability, and then value. (Women tend to see value emerging from the relationship.) She is looking for clues she can trust you the minute she walks in the door (See Chapter 5, "The Two-Minute Takeoff.") If trust is not there, the game is over before it begins, as far as the woman is concerned.

What a woman seeks in a caring relationship with her banker, insurance professional, financial adviser, or insurance sales professional is a little different from what a man looks for. Both, obviously, want to know that you will live up to your word, and that you have their best interests at heart. A woman, however, has some additional requirements:

- Can she rely on the strength of a personal relationship with you?

- Can she trust you as an ally to understand the pressures in her life and help her ease them?
- Can she rely on getting special treatment from you, if she needs it—not because she is a special person (or not *only* because she is a special person), but because she may be short of time and experience?

TRUST IS A FUNNY THING

Trust is a much-valued but often misunderstood quality. You demonstrate your trustworthiness over time, not all at once. Ultimately, it's up to other people to decide whether you're trustworthy or not.

Here are a few more things you need to know about trust:

- People make their decisions by carefully evaluating your behavior, not so much your grand gestures as how you behave in the smaller moments. That's why it takes a long time for trust to grow.
- Once someone trusts you, they no longer need further proof of your trustworthiness. They will then take your word, follow your advice, and accept your recommendations.
- However—and it's a BIG however—it takes only a moment to break this trust, and a long, long time to earn it back.

WHAT ABOUT MEN?

Don't men like special treatment, too? Sure they do. But for women it plays a bigger part in a satisfying buying experience.

THE 5 PRINCIPLES OF TRUST-BASED SELLING

We've organized into five principles everything you need to do to engender trust in your women clients:

Think relationship before product.

Respect her, her time, and her timing.

Understand her on her own terms.

Surpass her every expectation.

Telegraph confidence.

If you can internalize these principles and use them to shape your behavior, you'll have clients who will be open to your advice, stay with you through good times and bad, and tell so many of their friends how wonderful you are that you'll never have to make another cold call.

1. Think relationship before product

Because a woman relates more to people than to things, she finds it easier to connect with you than with the product you're selling. To her, the sales relationship comes before the sale. Whereas a man is looking for the best deal, a woman is looking for a total buying experience. You'll earn her trust (and her business) if you take the time to invest in getting to know her and letting her get to know you. There will be plenty of time to share your extensive product knowledge once you've established a connection. So slow down. Don't try to shoe-horn her into the timeframe that would work for a man.

WHAT THIS MEANS FOR YOU

If you can pace yourself to accommodate her process, you'll avoid frustration, and she'll relax and begin to feel more comfortable doing business with you.

HOW TO BRIDGE THE D-GENE

The challenge for most salespeople—men and women alike—is to shift their initial focus away from what they're selling. Although they may understand the importance of establishing a relationship with their clients, most salespeople do not realize just how "human" women clients need this relationship to be.

- *Allow time for her to get to know you—and you to get to know her.* When you're selling to a woman, expect a process rather than an event. Think of it as a trip from Point A to Point B: a man gets on an eight-lane interstate and is there in three hours. A woman takes the back roads and doesn't arrive for two days. That's because the woman wants to experience the trip itself so she can get comfortable with the new territory.

  You can't speed up her journey, so put it out of your mind. In the first place, if you spend all your time wishing she'd get on the Interstate, as a woman she's going to pick up the vibe that you're rushing her, even if you don't say anything. Secondly, you're going to lose out on the chance not only to build a strong relationship, but to learn things about her that will help you know what products or services to recommend.

> **THIS OLD THING?**
>
> *With greater powers of observation, you may even wise up to your spouse's habit of slipping new clothes past you. You know the one: "New? Oh no, Honey, I've had this dress for ages."*

- *Establish common ground.* This is different from the male practice of checking each other out to see who went to the better college, earns the higher salary, or drives the faster car. With women, the point is to find commonalities that will help bring you together as equals.

  Check to see what pastimes you share. Bring up community events she may have attended. See what she thinks of the new restaurant in town.

Don't be afraid to ask questions, but make sure you're not interrogating her. Lead with personal information of your own, and see if she responds. Pets and children (or grandchildren) resonate with almost everyone.

- *Notice what she may be carrying with her.* It could be a picture on a key chain, a travel brochure, or children's book. Use it to create a connection: "I couldn't help noticing the picture you have on your keychain. You must be a cat lover, too."

  The key here is to be observant. With the exception of people like Sherlock Holmes and Lt. Columbo, men aren't known for having an abundance of this trait; but with practice you'll be surprised how much you can pick up.
- *Remember her name and the names of the significant people in her life.* This may sound obvious, but it's especially important to women. If Julie calls you for some information, and you call her Jenny, she probably won't hang up on you, but you will have definitely lost some ground in earning her trust. On the other hand, if you can refer to her son or grandson by name, she will certainly think, and may even say, "Oh, you remembered!"
- *Act as her ally in the sales process.* Think of your organization's sales process. Where are the potential bottlenecks? Where's the red tape? Where are problems likely to arise? Remember, she's a busy person, and will appreciate anything you can do to help expedite the process for her. So don't just forget about her once you've made the sale. Help her understand what will happen next, and what additional papers she can expect to receive. Intercede on her behalf if a problem crops up. If she's looking for a special arrangement, or an exception to one of

DEMON MULTI-TASKERS

*In the same time it takes the **husband** to make the morning coffee, the **wife** will fix breakfast, pack the kids' lunches, write a shopping list, iron a shirt, call the office, find missing homework, and de-flea the cat.*

your rules, see what you can do to accommodate her. Your efforts will pay off in her trust—and in future sales from her and her friends.

2. Respect her, her time, and her timing

You can respect a woman client, first of all, by treating her with courtesy—not only the pull-her-chair-out-from-the-table kind but also the respectful deference that tells her she's the focus of your efforts. Second, you will never go wrong if you can always remember how short of time she is. By and large, women are a lot busier than men, especially working women. Women, with their ability to multi-task, are often given multiple responsibilities to juggle at work. And at home? Well, married working women still shoulder the bulk of family responsibilities. And being a single mom is not exactly a walk in the park.

TIME IS PRECIOUS TO WOMEN

- *63% of working women spend 40 hours or more on the job.*
- *40% of women 25 to 54 years old report that they have less than one hour a day for themselves.*

WHAT THIS MEANS FOR YOU

Because it's so important for women to feel they're being taken seriously, you can set yourself apart by going out of your way to extend respect. Quiet, focused forms of attention register big with women.

If you can support whatever decision-making approach your woman client wants to use—asking lots of questions, conferring with friends and family members, taking her time—you'll earn her respect, gratitude and future business.

HOW TO BRIDGE THE D-GENE

Your biggest challenge as a sales professional may be dealing with a woman's time pressures on the one hand, and, on the other, the time she needs to make a decision. To you, it might seem that the solution would be to help her decide faster. Here's a more effective approach:

- *Learn about her schedule and timeframe for making decisions.* When you're five or ten minutes late for a meeting with a male client, it's not good, but it's not the end of the world. A woman, on the other hand, may have planned her day so closely that she can't afford to lose this time. She may be paying a dollar for every minute she's late picking up her kid at child care. More important for your future relationship with her, a woman is much more likely than a man to take your lateness personally, as if you didn't respect her enough to make an effort to be on time.

- *Let your woman client set the pace each step of the way.* When you check with the woman before proceeding to the next step, you're showing respect by putting her in charge of the conversation.

  Make a conscious effort to say things that put the woman in charge, such as "Is that something you'd like to get into today?" or "When you're ready, I'd be happy to go over that with you."

  Avoid phrases like, "In order to save time, I'd like to…," "We need to make a decision soon so we don't lose out on this opportunity," or "Let's move on to the next point." And never look at your watch, unless it's to hurry yourself along.

TURN OFF YOUR PHONE

One woman we spoke to loves the fact that her broker always makes a point of turning off his cell phone during their meeting.

"I like the feeling that I don't have to compete for his attention," she says. "It makes me feel well cared for."

THE ULTIMATE SACRIFICE?

Letting the woman set the pace of the conversation is the equivalent of giving her the remote control.

Instead of saying "I hate to rush you, but I have another appointment," put the onus on yourself: "It looks like I haven't scheduled enough time for our meeting. Would you like to set up another one?"

- *Use your manners.* It's very simple: a lack of courtesy is a deal-breaker with women. So dust off your manners, and remember that women will notice how you treat other people. One woman reported having lunch with her banker, whom she observed taking a high-handed tone with the waiter. "It made me think less of her," she said.

  Because a woman may be more sensitive to being snubbed or excluded, avoid humor or topics of conversation she might not care about or be offended by.

  Wait to use nicknames until she invites you to. You don't want to run the risk of seeming pushy. (In this regard, you'll probably want to ask rather than assume that your relationship is on a first-name basis.)

3. Understand her on her own terms

For a woman, the goal of a conversation is to understand and to be understood as a person, not just in business terms. The point is not simply to trade information or establish dominance, as it often is for men.

As the D-gene tells us, women's natural ways of speaking and listening are different from men's. Women tend to avoid black-or-white statements. They use more qualifiers and disclaimers, in an effort to invite the other person into the conversation. Women also use more questions and upward inflections in order to see if the other person is in step with them.

Women expect to take turns when they talk, without having to fight to be heard. At times, women may appear hesitant or timid in conversation. In point of fact, these pauses are quite functional. Women are merely waiting to hear your response—and they would like you to do the same.

WHAT THIS MEANS FOR YOU

If you can modify your own conversational style to sync up with your women clients', you'll be letting them know that you're taking them seriously and tracking with them on both a business and more interpersonal level. If you can enter her world by being respectful of—and responsive to—her preferred conversational style, you'll get insights into her needs and decision-making rationale you could never otherwise hope for. For an insurance professional, this is golden information.

HOW TO BRIDGE THE D-GENE

Don't be surprised if this principle proves challenging. Women's and men's conversational styles—in fact, the dynamics of their interactions—are very different, as you saw in the last chapter. Men listen differently from women. They react much less. The first time we ever gave a presentation to an all-male audience, we thought we were bombing. They just sat there. Afterward, they had lots of questions and comments; it was obvious that they had been listening closely, but it didn't look that way to us. When we talk to groups of women, on the other hand, it can feel as if the building is about to take off. They smile, they nod, they gesture, they make comments to their friends. It's…well, it's different.

- *Value her conversation style.* Expect it to be more detailed and descriptive than what you will hear from men. If you can stop trying to net out what she's saying, or get her to cut to the chase, you'll learn a lot about who she is. And what sales representative doesn't need to know more about his or her clients?

- *Over-respond!* If women don't get frequent responses, they will assume you're not listening. So over-respond; it may feel forced at first, but you'll get used to it, and she'll get the picture that you're paying attention. By over-respond, we mean nodding, maintaining eye contact, dropping in some "uh-huhs" and "I sees," asking questions to learn more ("What was that like for you?"), and reflecting back her feelings ("You sound angry. I'd feel the same way if I were in your position.") (We'll have more to say on this topic in Chapter 6.)
- *Pay attention.* It bears repeating that a woman hates to talk to a man who is pretending to listen. You think women don't know that blank look when they see it? Think again. If you want to establish trusting relationships with your women clients, you may to need to come up with some strategies for tuning in. One man reported he pretended he'd be quizzed on everything his client was telling him.
- *Resist the temptation to interrupt.* We said it before and we'll say it again: Never interrupt. This a huge mistake on several levels: (1) it's rude, (2) it indicates you're not taking her seriously, (3) it increases her anxiety by making her feel she must compete to be heard, and (4) you're cutting her off from saying things that could be useful to you.

4. Surpass her every expectation

Although men certainly appreciate service above and beyond the call of duty, by and large your efforts to exceed expectations will have a bigger impact on women. It makes them feel special, it tells them you value the relationship, and it gives them the comfortable feeling that they are being well taken care of.

Finally, there's no better way to set yourself apart—and above—your competition.

There are two parts to this principle: first, the extra help you provide to make sure transactions go as smoothly as possible for her, and second, your thoughtful gestures that underscore the importance to you of the relationship.

Historically, women have pushed for more and better service— like stores staying open 24/7, for example. Once in place, however, these improvements appealed as much to men as they did to women.

WHAT THIS MEANS FOR YOU

Women have exceptional memories, and they like to share with other people. If you are able to do more for them than you promised—provide them with small extras even before they can think to ask for them—they'll reward you with their business, and also recommend you to their friends.

HOW TO BRIDGE THE D-GENE

The dual challenge for most salespeople is to remember how important this principle is for their women clients, and to be as creative as possible in going that extra mile. It's not about sending flowers or making the grand gesture. It's about knowing enough about her to do just the thing that will make her life a little happier and more hassle-free. In other words, this is where all that listening you've been doing can really pay off.

- *Attend to the details.* Making an effort to become more detailed-oriented can really pay off. If you call a client to make an appointment, and you're able to say, "I know Wednesday afternoons are out, because that's when you volunteer at the literacy project. How about Thursday?" she'll appreciate the fact that you remembered her schedule.

If you have a hard time even remembering your own wedding anniversary, you may want to think about getting some help. Is there someone in your office who can make sure you keep track of things? An electronic tickler file you could set up?

- *Under-promise and over-deliver.* It's always safer to take the conservative path. In the first place, a woman doesn't like people who toot their own horns, and if you make outlandish promises, that's what she'll think. Secondly, when you can't deliver, you not only disappoint her, you add seeds of doubt about just how important she is to you, and how trustworthy you are overall. So if the check won't come for two weeks, tell her that, and then do whatever you can to get it there faster.

- *Do everything you can to make her life easier.* If something has gone wrong for her, step in, and fix it. If the screw-up is somewhere in your own organization, find out who's responsible. Follow up, and let her know what you're doing. (We'll have more to say about this in Chapter 9.)

- *Surprise her with unexpected human gestures.* We know an insurance salesman who always brings a little goodie with him to client meetings. How about keeping some cookies in your office to go with the coffee? Send her a newspaper clipping that relates to something she told you. You're letting her know that she's important enough for you to have listened—and remembered. When you send a greeting card or follow-up note, do you use the company stationery, or do you take the trouble to pick out a nice card you

The best salespeople think of themselves as friends of their clients. The help they offer does not always have a lot to do with insurance.

think she would like? (We'll explore this topic in much greater detail in Chapter 10.)

5. Telegraph confidence

A woman wants a qualified and reliable ally in the sales process, someone who projects both confidence and competence. If you come across as anything less than capable and trustworthy, women clients will pick it up. For this reason, it's important to be fully aware of the verbal and nonverbal messages you send.

WHAT THIS MEANS FOR YOU

When everything about you conveys a sense of confidence that is genuine and compelling, women clients react by placing their trust in you.

HOW TO BRIDGE THE D-GENE

The biggest challenge for sale professionals—for everyone, really—is to *feel* confident so you can *project* confidence. On the other hand, you can feel confident and still send out messages women will interpret differently, especially when they first meet you.

- *Develop a deep reservoir of product knowledge.* Increased product knowledge breeds self-confidence. If you get into situations where you feel as if you're winging it, go back and do some more homework. Remember, the point is not to overwhelm your client with product details, but to develop enough product knowledge to feel confident you can handle any situation. Your confidence is what she's looking for.

- *Smile.* A smile is one of a sales rep's greatest under-used tools. There's no more powerful way to let your customers know you're at ease and feeling good about what you're doing.
- *Behave confidently.* Did you know that research shows that if you behave confidently, you'll come to feel more confident? (This is known in some circles as the "fake it 'til you make it" rule.) Your mother had it right: stand up straight. Don't slouch. Develop a firm (as versus bone-crushing) handshake. Look the other person in the eye. Don't mumble. Speak clearly with an upbeat tone in your voice.

You need to bring these principles into play in all the work you do with your women clients; but there is one time when they absolutely have to be front and center, and that's during what we call the Two-Minute Takeoff.

5 THE TWO-MINUTE TAKEOFF

Hitting on All Five Principles

Let's take a moment to review where we are. You learned about just how big the women's market is for life insurance, annuities, and long-term care insurance. You learned about the D-gene: how men and women are different, and why an understanding of the difference matters to your success. We talked about five principles you can follow that will help you demonstrate your trustworthiness, which is the first thing women look for in a sales professional, as in, if she doesn't trust you, you're toast.

OK. You've absorbed all that, in a cerebral sort of way, and are about to have a conversation with a client of the feminine persuasion. You've spoken briefly on the phone. Now she's at your office door. Or you're knocking on her front door. What do you do next?

Maybe you should wing it. After all, you no doubt already have experience working with clients—maybe a lot. However, what if someone told you that within the first two minutes of meeting you, a woman will decide whether or not you are someone she can do business with?

And here's something else to think about: when a woman meets you for the first time, she may already have some half-conscious preconceptions about you, based on her prior experiences with other people in sales. You know what they are, right? The concern that you won't take her seriously. That you'll take advantage of her relative lack of financial experience. And if you're a man, that you might even make a pass.

Not fair, you say? You're right, it isn't, but that's the way life is sometimes.

Your first task is not to take this personally. These preconceptions are not about you, specifically. You may be the most D-gene-savvy person on the planet, but you as you are someone who sells for a living, you come with a certain amount of baggage. And we'll say it clearly—if you are male, your load of baggage could be sizeable.

BUT WHAT IF SHE DOESN'T FEEL THIS WAY?

Act as if she does, and you can't go wrong.

First of all, she probably does feel this way to some extent— even if she's very successful in her own field, and even if she seems totally in charge.

Besides, these behaviors are all common sense. They just happen to be more important to women than to men.

Does this mean she's a raging feminist? Absolutely not. Does she have a chip on her shoulder? Not at all. Let's just say that she's got very good reasons to be alert to any signs that she's not being taken seriously.

If you are a female sales associate, does any of this apply? Not in any gender-related way, of course, but the underlying anxiety and distrust may still be there. Read on to find out more.

Obviously you'll want to make sure you are observing each of the five principles of trust-based selling in your first meeting. But you'll never get a second chance to make a first impression, as the saying goes. So, we've put together the *Maddox Smye Never-Fail Steps to a Successful Two-Minute Takeoff.* Very short and sweet. Ready?

Step 1. Go to her. Don't make her come to you.

Why? Think back to when you were in high school and you had to walk across the gym floor to ask a girl or a guy to dance. How did you feel? Exposed? Vulnerable? Unsure of yourself? She's feeling a little like that now. It's up to you to create a safe environment in which she can open up and start sharing the reason for her visit. The safer and more comfortable she feels, the easier it will be for you to create the kind of relationship she's looking for—one that will result in increased sales.

Step 2. Shake her hand.

Women are touchier—in the sense of liking to touch—than men. On the other hand, any touching between the sexes in the workplace these days is generally a bad idea, especially if it's initiated by a man—except for the handshake. So take the initiative. Don't wait for her to offer her hand; in the business world we've gone beyond that bit of Victorian etiquette. This is all about extending yourself, so extend your hand and shake hers firmly. If you're a man, shake her hand in much the way you would shake a man's hand, remembering, of course, that your hand is probably bigger than hers and your grip may be stronger.

Step 3. Introduce yourself—slowly.

You probably already know that whenever people approach a discussion of their finances, their anxiety level goes up—sometimes way up. Anxious people can't listen very well. As a money manager once told us, "When it comes to talking to clients about their money, I've gotten used to saying everything three times."

So take your time when you tell her your name, especially if it's a mouthful. Give her a card so she can read it. Names are often easier to understand when people can see them.

Step 4. Maintain eye contact and SMILE.

Women make and maintain eye contact more than men. That's part of the D-gene, as you learned in Chapter 3. Watch a man who is introduced to someone, male or female. Very shortly after meeting, his eyes will begin to shift—to other people in the room, to a picture on the wall, to his shoes, to nothing much at all. To a woman, this behavior literally looks shifty, and makes her wonder what he's really thinking. (We assume we don't need to explain a woman's reaction to a man who does his eye shifting up and down her body.)

If you find it hard to sustain eye contact, do what actors do: focus on one eye, or pick a spot between the other person's eyes and concentrate on that.

Don't forget to smile. When you smile upon first meeting a client, you're conveying a lot: I'm happy to meet you, I like what I'm doing, I feel confident that I can help you and that we will work well together. You probably can't fake a smile—not one you'd want anybody to see—but you can encourage the kinds of positive, upbeat feelings that will make you feel like smiling. So make the effort to put yourself in a positive mood: a genuine smile is hard to resist.

Step 5. Offer refreshments.

Research shows that the more senses you can engage, the stronger the connection you can create. What creates a stronger connection than sharing food or a beverage?

If she's come to your place of business, stale office coffee won't impress her. How about some special blends, or a selection of exotic teas? Do you have some halfway decent cups and saucers? Nice paper napkins? Soft drinks? Cookies? Candies? Get things set up now, and you'll be ready when she arrives.

Also: if you can serve the refreshments yourself—instead of calling on a female assistant—you'll be way ahead of the game. Sad to say, women are seldom served by men. When they are, it makes a big impression.

If you're calling on her at her home, why not bring some

interesting goodies to eat or drink? Scout around your community for high-end delis or food emporiums that sell interesting pastries that can be elegantly wrapped.

That's it. Five simple steps to a two-minute takeoff. We told you it wouldn't take long.

Now you're ready to move into the sales conversation itself.

6 MASTERING THE ART OF FEMALE-FOCUSED LISTENING

How to Uncover Her Unique Needs and Wants

"You're not listening!"

If the average man pocketed a nickel for each time he got this complaint from a woman, his pants would fall down.

Let's face it, guys. You are notorious for not listening to women, even women clients. You know you're supposed to—they're clients, after all—but still you find yourself tuning out. Why? If you're being honest, you'll probably admit to one or more of these reasons:

> **HUSBAND'S NOTE TO HIS WIFE**
>
> *Someone from the Guyna Colleges called.*
>
> *They said the Pabst Beer is normal.*
>
> *I didn't know you liked beer.*

- I know in 45 seconds what she needs.
- I've heard it all before.
- I've heard it all before *from her.*
- I know what she means.
- I know what she's trying to say.
- Most of what she's saying is irrelevant.

No wonder one of the first questions men ask in our workshops is not, "How can I learn to listen better?," but "How can I get her to shut up?"

These men don't like our answer—which is "you can't"—until they realize how they can turn this initial part of the sales process into the beginning of a profitable buying and selling partnership.

So, let's assume you've successfully achieved a Two-Minute Takeoff with a woman client. What's your next move? (Choose one of the following.)

A. Lock in her initial interest by making sure she knows your stellar qualities as a salesman who is D-gene-certified.

B. Ask her what she's looking for.

C. Ask how you can help her make the best use of her time.

You probably said "C," because you figured the correct answer to multiple-choice questions like these is usually the third choice. You're right, but do you know *why?*

The answer goes back to the second principle of trust-based selling: Respect her, her time, and her timing. By asking her how you can make the best use of her time, you're showing respect for the fact that she probably has every minute of her day accounted for and you want to make sure you don't take too much of her time.

The interview process that's typically used with first-time clients of insurance products is male-oriented. By that, we mean it is built around the concept of screening, of eliminating extraneous information, of quickly zeroing in on the main points, the key facts, the action items. This process reveals men's preference for arriving quickly at a narrow focus, and organizing information around that focus.

The form below shows the type and order of information on a typical insurance industry needs analysis form. You can see how tempting it is to simply take the client through the items and write down what he or she says.

"HELP" OR "HELPFUL"?

Do you know why "How can I be most helpful to you today?" is a better question than "How can I help you today?"

Because the first question focuses on how you can serve her, while the second implies that she's weak and needs help.

Small point? Maybe, but small points add up.

Client Name: *Date:*

Personal Information: age, date of birth, children, etc.

Annual income

Other types of insurance: company, face amount, premium, expiration date

Assets and liabilities

ASSETS	**LIABILITIES**
Savings	*Rent*
Checking	*Auto Loan*
IRA's	*Credit Cards*
Mutual Funds	*Other Loans*
Stock	*Mortgage*
Retirement plan	

Spouse's annual income:

Total annual income your family would need if you died today

Number of years your spouse expects to work?

Number of children, need for college tuition and expenses

Goals/Concerns:

1. ______________________ 4. ______________________

2. ______________________ 5. ______________________

3. ______________________ 6. ______________________

Notes:

____

____

____

____

WHAT SHE'S LOOKING FOR

Are you "merely" doing a good job, or do you really care about what she's telling you?

This is not the preferred process for most women, even though they may have no trouble going along with it. If left to their own devices, however, many women would start with the notes section. (Once they start talking, this is probably what they'll do anyway, so you might as well relax and enjoy the ride.)

If a man likes to focus, a woman likes to share. To make a good decision, she wants to know the whole picture, and she thinks that you, as her insurance person, should, too. So when you take her through your series of screening questions, she's perfectly capable of answering them, but they make her a little anxious: are you really listening to her? Are you getting her situation? Do you understand the dynamics of her life enough to make the kinds of recommendations that will suit her best?

In other words, women don't want to answer yes-or-no questions. They want you to understand their lives, not because they think they're so fascinating, but because this is the kind of information they'd want if they were in your position.

FEELING FINDER

One sales professional we spoke to said she created a "feeling finder" form to elicit a client's priorities, concerns, and future security issues.

That's at the level of information. At another level, sharing information is part of a woman's way of building a relationship. She's telling you about her family, or her work, or her goals and concerns, as a way of establishing common ground. As one saleswoman with a lot of women clients put it, "When you work with a woman, you establish a relationship not just with her but with everything in her life that she takes care of, worries about, or feels responsible for."

Meanwhile, of course, your clock is ticking. You have appointments. You have sales goals. The day is going by. As she talks, you may find yourself getting antsy and your attention wandering: How long is this going to take? What does she want from me? I wonder if the Lakers won?

Fair enough: you've got your agenda, and she's got hers. The only thing is that she is the client. Here's what we're saying: if you can find a way to tune in to her—*her* way—you'll be well rewarded.

In this chapter, we're going to tell you four things you can do to uncover her unique needs and wants in a female-focused way. Before we get started, however, you need to let go of any previous plans or preconceptions you may have had about the meeting's outcome. Think of what you're doing in this conversation as beginning a process, not working towards a specific outcome. The more you discuss her life situation, the more she may realize that she has multiple needs that exceed the immediate reason for contacting you.

SLOW DOWN.

You're not barreling down the Interstate. You're touring the local roads—and learning a great deal about your client as you go.

Taking the time to get to know her and her expectations will help establish your credibility. It shows her you value her and the relationship as much as you do a sale, and gives her the confidence of knowing your recommendations will be uniquely suited to her special needs and circumstances.

1. TAP INTO HER STORY

Most salespeople are trained by their companies to take prospective clients through a series of qualifying questions. In our seminars, people often ask us for a standard list of screening questions geared to women. "It doesn't have to be long," one young man said. "In fact, it's better if it's short, on one side of the page, so I can have it in my lap or top desk drawer to refer to."

Sorry, guys. What you're looking for just doesn't fit the D-gene. Instead, you need to be prepared for a wide-ranging back-and-forth conversation, with lots of detours and digressions. It might not seem very organized, from a man's point of

"No longer are clients and producers motivated by the single transaction. That's why a holistic view toward helping clients address their changing needs over the course of their lifetimes is critical in today's world."

Clayton Wilson, *"Understanding the Women's Market,"* Broker World, *March 2005*

view, but if you commit to tracking with her you'll hear most of what you need for both your immediate and future use.

Here are some topics and brief excerpts from the conversation of a woman at her first meeting with an insurance professional. (Note that she was referred to him by one of his other women clients. As we said, once a woman decides you're trustworthy, she'll tell everyone about you.)

I got your name from Rosemary, a friend of mine whose husband also lost his job, like mine has. We've got two kids, both in high school, and I'm concerned that in our reduced circumstances their college opportunities are going to be severely limited... when Frank lost his job, he lost a whole package—pension, life insurance. We're coping, but barely. Frank is working at a hardware store while he interviews for something in his field. I'm trying to start up my interior decorating business again. But without life insurance I feel really vulnerable if anything should happen. Frank says everything will be okay, that we just have to get through this period, but I'm not sleeping.

If you can forget for a moment about what she's not telling you—her assets, her liabilities, her budget, etc., and tune into what she is saying, you'll pick up a treasure trove of information you can use now and in the future to provide the kind of proactive service that will result in increased sales. Some examples of proactive service:

1. Give her your home or cell phone number, so she can always reach you.

2. Offer to discuss affordable options for life insurance that will alleviate her worries—either with her or with her and her husband.

3. Send some brochures about products that would help her and her husband save for tuition payments.
4. Describe the benefits that might be available to her as a female owner of a small business, and offer to put her in touch with someone who might be able to help her explore these possibilities.
5. Give her the names of small business associations in the area she might want to hook up with.

Before you start asking questions, there are a few key steps you need to take. First, explain that you're going to be seeking information about her situation that will help you make the best possible recommendations for her. Let her know that you'll be taking notes, and that she should feel free to interrupt at any time if she has a question.

The questions you ask should not be intended to make you look smart. Their purpose is to get her talking about what she wants and needs.

In order to do the best job for you, I need to know what's important to you. So I'll be asking questions, and taking notes on what you say. If you have questions at any point in this process, please ask. That's part of my job.

Ask how you can be most helpful to her at this meeting. Clarify how much time she has.

How can we make the best use of your time right now?

Start with the broad, open-ended questions. Be sure to include questions that allow her to tell you about issues of importance in her life.

What would you say are your priorities and concerns?

How do you see your situation now?

What would you like to accomplish, personally and professionally, for yourself and your family?

What will it take for you to feel secure in the future?

What expectations do you have of me and my organization?

Chances are she won't have sound-byte answers to any of these questions. Instead she'll do what most of us do, men as well as women, which is to use the process of answering to think through what she means, adding layers of context as she talks. You can strengthen your connection with her by creating a judgment-free zone in which she can think through her needs, asking for your advice when she needs it.

2. STAY TUNED INTO HER

You don't simply need to pay attention. You need to show her that you're paying attention.

This is another one of those D-gene moments. Men and women behave differently when they're listening. Men may not make eye contact. They may look distracted, or out the window, or lost in thought. They may have a frown on their faces. None of this means they're not listening; quite the contrary, they may be concentrating deeply.

When women are listening, on the other hand, they don't just sit there. They make eye contact. They nod. They *respond.* They *react physically.* They share their own experiences in an effort to draw the other person closer. All this, to a woman, is listening. What a man does is...something else, she's not quite sure what. Since she's already anxious about not being taken seriously, it's easy for her to leap to conclusions when she sees you just sitting there. Maybe you're bored, she thinks. Maybe you think she's stupid. Maybe you're just waiting to contradict her.

Your challenge, therefore, is to pay attention *visibly*. Show her you're listening. Demonstrate your interest through eye contact, head nods, voice tone, and short phrases.

SHE: *Last Thursday night at 10:30 I was on my cell phone, waiting for my luggage at the Pittsburgh airport while my assistant read me a draft of a press release that had to go out the next day. That's crazy.*

YOU: *Ten-thirty?! I'm brain-dead at ten-thirty.*

SHE: *Me too! That's why I have to get off this merry-go-round.*

YOU: *Sounds like you're thinking of retiring sooner rather than later.*

SHE: *You know…I think you're right.*

YOU: *Yeah. You sound ready.*

SHE: *I am! I am good and ready! Let's take another look at those annuities.*

Listen with your eyes as well as your ears. What message are her body language and facial expressions giving you? Is it different from what she's saying? You may want to comment on the discrepancy directly:

YOU: *You mentioned the peace of mind of knowing your sister is looking in on your parents, but you still seem concerned.*

Or you may want to tuck this information away, so that, for example, you have some long-term care insurance recommendation ready if she changes her mind.

3. ASK HER QUESTIONS TO CLARIFY MEANING, FEELINGS, AND DETAILS

Once she's answered your broad questions, you'll need to sift and sort through what she's told you in order to tailor a solution that's best for her. The more you can link your questions back to something specific she said, or an emotional state, the more she'll realize that you were really listening. Here are some clarifying questions you can ask:

You said you need to do something right away. What's your time frame?

What happened to make that experience so frustrating for you?

What sum of money would give you that sense of security you're looking for?

Make sure your questions reflect your need for clarification or for more information, rather than any suggestion that she's not expressing herself clearly. Since women tend to be self-deprecating, you may need to go out of your way not to give this impression.

Make it as easy as possible for her to provide information. Many people, men as well as women, resist thinking about any kind of insurance, especially life or long-term care insurance. They approach the subject the same way they approach getting in shape: they mean to, they know it's important, but somehow they always find an excuse for avoiding it. You may well get partial answers to your questions about assets, obligations, and their future goals. You may need to sit down with your client and a shoebox full of records to help her figure out her areas of exposure and how to handle them. This is the information you'll need, now or later, to explore products to handle multiple needs.

4. CONVEY YOUR UNDERSTANDING SO SHE KNOWS SHE'S BEEN HEARD

Women want to know they've been correctly understood. They want to make sure you got the facts, but they also want to know you understand the important nuances of their situation. So at key points in your discussion, play back your understanding of the facts and how she feels about them.

So in your new position you're going to be traveling a lot and won't be available to look after your parents if one should get sick, even though ideally that's what you'd like to do.

You need to make sure your understanding is accurate, because it will become the basis of the subsequent work you do with her.

Don't be surprised if you don't get it right the first time. She may have given you a great deal of big-picture information to process, and it may take you some time to extract the meaning she intended. Don't let this bother you. This kind of collaborative process is embedded in the D-gene. Besides, there are benefits of not getting it right the first time:

- She gets to explain some more, which translates into more bonding.
- She gets to correct you, which if it doesn't happen too often, will make you seem more human to her. Besides, what woman doesn't like to correct a man?

By the same token, she may well change her mind when she hears your summary. What's important is not what she told you but the understanding you eventually arrive at together.

Pitfalls

- *Don't short-circuit the process by telling her what she wants.* You may be right. After all, this is your job, and you speak to clients every day. Even so, you're robbing the client of the ability to crystallize her thoughts and share them with you. You're also neglecting the relationship-building that happens when she tells you her story.

- *Don't pepper her with questions.* You're not a trial lawyer, and she's not a hostile witness. Avoid series of closed questions, especially those that call for a yes or no answer. After you ask a question, give her plenty of time to answer. Add your reactions to what she said before you jump in with the next question.
- *Avoid leading questions.* Women are especially sensitive to questions that seem to manipulate or patronize. "You want to save money, don't you?" or "I'm sure you'd agree that…" fall into this category.
- *Keep your distance.* Avoid a listening stance that leans into her personal space and makes her feel threatened.
- *Don't interrupt.* If you think we're repeating ourselves on this topic, it's because we are.
- *Don't be afraid of silence.* You don't want to just sit there till she says something. After all, you're not a psychoanalyst. Still, a few gentle silences will have the effect of encouraging her to open up, especially if you then respond with nods, and phrases of understanding.

The Next Phase

If everything has been going well, you've reached a common understanding about what your client wants. You've begun to feel more comfortable with each other as you have shown your respect and interest in her as a person rather than just a client. Now you're ready to move on to the next phase in the process, which is offering recommendations that you think will best meet her insurance needs.

Don't be surprised if you don't move to this phase at the end of your first meeting, or even your second. It's part of the

D-gene to be very thorough and to talk to other people about you to see what they think.

She'll let you know when she's ready. At this point, you need to move from a fairly free-wheeling conversation to a discussion of solutions: products, services, recommendations. Your challenge will be to make this shift without leaving behind the conversational, collaborative tone you have worked hard to establish.

7 TURNING YOUR PRESENTATION INTO A CONVERSATION

How to Share the Information She Wants, the Way She Wants It

One of the things we love most about good sales professionals is their enthusiasm for the product or service they're selling. It's a pleasure to deal with people who are passionate about their work, and convinced that what they are selling is exactly what you need. Can you imagine making a major purchase from someone who lacks this quality?

Probably not. However...

Early on in the selling process, your clients—and especially your women clients—aren't ready for any heavy-duty selling. Women appreciate your passion, but what they're really after at this point is information—and not just any information, either, but information that responds specifically to their concerns. Otherwise, they're likely to think they're being hustled. Of course, men don't like to be hustled either, but they are usually able to dismiss it as part of the selling game. Women, on the other hand, tend to take it personally...does this person really think I'm stupid enough to buy this line of bull? If they think they're being hustled, they're likely to leave and never come back.

What this means is, if you had planned to give a canned presentation to your woman client, you might want to rethink your plan. Your challenge instead is to maintain the conversational approach that you adopted when you were asking her about her needs, and still give her the information and/or recommendations she needs to make a decision.

Canned Presentations? Who, Me?

The ability to shift seamlessly from asking about her needs to offering information or making recommendations about your product is the hallmark of trusted advisers. It's a natural shift for them because they don't have the "now it's time to sell her something" mind-set. They see the whole experience in terms of constantly refining their knowledge of the client—first of her needs, and then of how best to match their products with those needs.

Even though you may not make what you think of as a canned presentation, as an experienced sales professional you probably have certain approaches and patterns of speech—phrases or even whole paragraphs—that you have found effective when talking with clients about your products and services. Since in all probability most of your clients have been men, you may want to reexamine some of these "sure-fire" lines and techniques in light of how effective they are with women.

Here's a quick quiz to help you conduct an inventory:

	YES	NO
1. I use a lot of sports and military analogies.		
2. I typically present information for three minutes or more without interruption.		

	YES	NO
3. I focus more on features than on benefits.		
4. I add value by making strong recommendations, since I'm more aware of the consequences of these decisions than most of my clients.		
5. Although I don't make canned presentations, I do rely on a few key slides to explain my product or service.		
6. To move clients along, I sometimes use phrases like "you'll never go wrong…," "this opportunity won't last forever…" and "you can trust me when I tell you…"		
7. I use a lot of humor to make my points.		
8. I use phrases like "If you're like most people…"		
9. I describe benefits in terms of increased status, e.g., "this will help you really stand out from the crowd."		
10. I use a lot of directive terms: "you should," "you'll have to," and "you need to."		

None of these approaches is D-gene-friendly, with the possible exception of humor. We include it here because the particular humor that has proven effective with male clients might not necessarily work well with women.

People in our training seminars frequently ask us about prepared presentations aimed at women. If a standard version works with men, they want to know, why couldn't someone put together a presentation that was D-gene-friendly?

First of all, we question whether prepared presentations are as effective with men as many sales professionals think. Leaving that aside, just as we've never seen a workable standard screening set of questions, we've never come across a scripted presentation that works terribly well with a woman client. One reason is that a woman has too many questions that take the presenter too far afield for a single script to be much of a guide. A bigger reason, however, is that a woman is looking for a unique solution that responds specifically to what she told you; the slightest whiff of something canned will cause her to question just how much you really understand her needs.

So if you can't use your salesman shtick, what's left? Four skills that will enable you to give her the information she wants without undercutting your role as a trusted adviser.

1. MAKE IT A TWO-WAY STREET

Men, you'll remember, talk in longer chunks of time than women do. Women talk in shorter chunks, and they also take turns talking by pausing to give the other person a chance to step in. But realistically speaking, at this point you may have more to tell her than she has to tell you (although if you haven't done a good job of listening, this may not be true). So what do you do?

First, ask her what information she wants and the best way for you to provide it. The idea is to make sure she stays in charge of the process at all times. The following comparison illustrates the difference between telling her what she needs to know and putting her in the driver's seat.

GENERIC APPROACH	D-GENE-FRIENDLY APPROACH
It's a really solid policy. I'd recommend it to anybody.	What would you like to know about this policy?
Remind me before you leave to give you a packet of information.	Would you like a couple of articles to read? Or would you like me to set up a meeting with...
There are basically three things you need to know about this policy.	What features of this policy should we go over?

Of course, you'll still need to make sure that she gets all the information she needs to make an informed decision.

These are the issues I see. Would you agree? Which are most important from your perspective?

What we're talking about here is a matter of emphasis: start with what *she* wants to know, instead of what you think she needs to know.

Answer her questions when she asks them, not when you would like to answer them. If you're one of those methodical people who eat all your peas and then all your mashed potatoes, even the thought of following this guideline could drive you crazy. All we're saying is, the more you can do to get on your client's wavelength, the greater your chances of increasing your immediate sale, and the potential for additional sales down the road. It's your choice.

WHAT'S YOUR MENTAL IMAGE?

Instead of thinking of a presentation as giving a speech, imagine that you are an expert witness in a trial, being questioned by a friendly lawyer.

Give brief, concise answers to her questions, and then ask her what else she'd like to know. You're the product expert, and it's tempting to take her question and run with it. Keep in mind, however, that while you may be the product expert, you're not the expert at knowing what she wants. As a general rule, you probably shouldn't talk for more than a minute or two without giving her an opportunity to respond.

HOW TO PATRONIZE AND DISCOUNT A CUSTOMER

"What a great question! I'll get to it in just a minute."

Check in with her periodically to see if she's getting what she wants. You're not looking for a grade on your performance. You know she's on a tight schedule, and you want to make sure she's getting the information she needs to make a decision.

It's important to determine how she prefers to learn. Is it by reading? Listening? Seeing a visual? Many people—including many women—respond well to stories of people like themselves and how the product you're selling has solved a problem for them or improved their lives.

Until you know what kind of learner she is, try different approaches. Watch her face and see if she responds. If she seems uninterested in a factual explanation, you might say, "Here's another way to look at it," and put the information in story form.

2. TAKE WHAT YOU'VE LEARNED FROM HER AND USE IT

There's nothing more effective than linking back everything you say about your product or service to something she told you. It's a good selling practice in general, but it's especially effective when used with women.

This is another place where all the careful listening you did will pay off, by enabling you to make close links between what your product can do and what she has told you she wants:

This investment will pay enough to cover the mortgage on that cabin in the woods you were telling me about.

This annuity means you can stop worrying about having to move to Minnesota to live with your son.

I took this approach because I know your work doesn't leave you much time to keep track of these things.

Here are some things you can do to let her know you're basing your suggestions and recommendations on what she told you:

- Refer to the notes you took.
- Use her exact words or phrases whenever possible. It's a good way to demonstrate your respect.
- Underscore any outcomes she feels strongly about.
  This will increase your post-retirement income, which I know is important to you.

- If you're offering a range of suggestions, prioritize them based on what you've learned is important to her.

  Since you said you'll continue to consult for several years after your formal retirement…

- Use technical terms that match her level of knowledge and understanding.
- Select visual support, sales and marketing materials she'll find relevant and useful to share with others.

SIMPLIFY SIMPLIFY

Insurance products can be very complex. Your challenge is to simplify the features, but without withholding information that will make the woman suspect you're flimflamming. If you lose her trust, you're toast.

- Paint word pictures that help make your point.

  I'm aware of your not wanting to get bogged down in details. I want you to feel like you're getting a high-level view; as if you were looking down at the market from a hot-air balloon.

- Be enthusiastic about the solution you're recommending.

Of course, it goes without saying that clients also convey information about what they need less directly. If you've been tuning into her body language and tone of voice as well as her words, you may have picked up some unspoken concerns or fears. It's probably more effective to acknowledge these indirectly:

> *Many people are concerned about their ability to make the right decisions at the right time. The suggestions we're talking about today will free you up from that worry.*

3. POSITION THE TOTAL CLIENT EXPERIENCE TO HER

Few if any of the products you sell are unique to you or your organization. If you want to distinguish yourself from your competition, you need to demonstrate other ways you can add value. One of the strongest differentiators, especially for women, is the post-sale service you and members of your team provide to make the experience as easy for her as you can. Make sure you relate the services provided to any unique needs of hers, keeping in mind that her greatest need is probably for more time.

Here's my cell phone number. You can always reach me on it.

Assuming we move forward, you'll be getting a lot of paperwork associated with what we've been planning today. If you like, you can bring it in here and we can sort it out for you.

4. MAKE YOUR NETWORK HER NETWORK

One of your greatest assets is your roster of other satisfied clients. Consider them your fan club, and don't be afraid to call on them. If a woman client has some concerns or objections, tell stories about satisfied clients who had similar concerns at first. Offer to put her in contact with clients who would be willing to share their experiences. Giving her the chance to share her situation and learn from others is a very D-gene-friendly way to resolve concerns. It removes you from the expert role, and enables her to get a sense of the kind of person you are from other clients.

Pitfalls

Here are some behaviors to avoid when you're sharing information about your product or service:

- *Bad-mouthing the competition.* It's not a good idea under any circumstances, but women find it especially objectionable. How can they be sure that you won't bad-mouth them behind their backs?

- *Bragging.* Women are very suspicious of overt bragging. But don't worry. If you make sure your plaques, certificates, and awards are prominently displayed in your office, these inanimate objects will do your bragging for you.

- *"Talking down."* The trick here is to examine your assumptions. If you assume that women "can't understand figures" or "don't get technology," you need to update your thinking. Everyone learns and understands differently. One way is not better or worse than any other. (We won't bore you with the women who have made fortunes understanding figures and "getting" technology.) Keep in mind that the more you can adapt to your clients' preferences, the greater your chances of increasing your sales.

- *Lecturing.* Don't use her question or comment to launch into a lecture. Keep it conversational. Remember, her head-nodding means that she hears you, not that she agrees with you. If she does too much nodding, you're doing too much talking.

- *Humor.* Guys banter and rib each other as a way to make contact. Many women don't like it, so don't do it.

8 MAKING THE SALE HER WAY

How to Complete a Pressure-less Close

Let's be frank. No matter how much effort you put into creating a trust-based relationship with a client, the fact remains that as a sales professional you make your living closing deals. Absolutely nothing wrong with that. Our whole purpose is to help you close more deals. The only problem is that the classic closing techniques, which are based primarily on manipulation ("What color should we order that in?"), don't work very well with women.

When it comes to closing, most salespeople know that clients don't like a hard sell, and they try not to appear too aggressive. If the client is a woman, they may make an extra effort. Yet when they reach the point of wanting to close and the woman isn't ready, or doesn't *seem* ready, their good intentions can fly out the window, and they're suddenly all over her—pushing and pressuring her for a decision. The result? What had looked like a sure thing suddenly turns very, very cold.

WHEN A WOMAN LEAVES

When women meet with a salesperson, they always go in with an exit strategy—I've got to pick up my son from soccer practice, or I'm meeting a friend in 30 minutes. That way, if the meeting doesn't go well, they can leave without a confrontation or hurt feelings. The problem for the salesperson is that he may have lost a client without ever knowing why.

Closing a deal can be a stressful experience. You've invested time in the client, and you want it—you need it—to pay off. The greater your need, the greater the temptation to shift your focus from serving the client to making the sale, even though you may know better. During periods of stress it's not unusual to fall back on old behaviors, even if you've come to believe they're not effective, simply because they're familiar. That's why, in your focus on closing, you might forget everything you've learned about the D-gene and default to high-pressure mode—which doesn't have to be very high to turn women off.

A Classic Tale

That's what happened to Alex, a financial services provider who had started out selling a life insurance policy to a woman and had then gotten into helping her take a look at her finances with a view towards retiring in about 10 years. He had presented several annuities for her consideration, and he thought she had made her choice. Things were going well until the day he went for the close. Here is how he described the situation:

> *It was that last meeting when it all went off the tracks. At the first meeting she had brought up the idea of doing some retirement planning. She had assembled some financial information about herself. She asked about annuities and I said I could send her some information. So I did, and she had some questions, and I came back to her house and we discussed her possible choices.*
>
> *She seemed very pleased, but said she wanted to talk things over with her brother, so we scheduled a third meeting. My understanding was I'd be closing the sale at that time.*
>
> *This third meeting took place the last week of the month. Frankly, I hadn't had a very good month, so I was looking forward to getting her signed up. Her son-in-law liked the plan; I thought his approval was the final piece of the puzzle. She had more questions, but she seemed to agree with all the answers I gave her.*

When I showed her the papers she had to sign, which I had already drawn up, she nodded in agreement, but eventually she said she wanted to talk to a few more people. Apparently her chiropractor didn't like annuities, and she wanted to hear what he had to say.

Her chiropractor!¿ I didn't say anything, but it really made me mad that she would equate a chiropractor with a trained financial adviser. Anyway, I didn't want to spend any more time with her if she wasn't serious, so I started asking her some questions to find out where she stood. I figured if she didn't sign something before the end of the meeting, I'd lose her. Right away she starts backing off and saying she needs more time, and she's running late, and 'don't call me, I'll call you.'

So that's that. I guess she was just shopping around.

What Went Wrong

Of course, we don't know how Alex's client experienced this process, but we've heard enough versions of this story to make a guess. Although Alex may have started out the selling process doing a lot of listening and giving her plenty of choices, as the month wore on (and it wasn't a good month for him) he began to get concerned or maybe even desperate. Based on his experience with other clients (mostly male) he figured she should have made up her mind by now. This, plus the fact that she wanted to talk to more people (including her chiropractor¿!) made him suspect she wasn't really interested. So he started pushing—to test her sincerity, to get her to commit, to meet his quota—and that's when he lost her.

In this part of the selling process it's very easy for someone who doesn't understand the D-gene to misread or ignore a woman's signals, and as a result end up losing the sale.

In this case, the salesman's gut instinct that she was ready to buy was based on his experience with male clients. Also, as you now know, all her nodding meant only that she understood what he was saying, not that she agreed with it. Finally, when she said she wanted to think about it and talk to her chiropractor, she was not sending a "no interest" message. Research into the D-gene indicates that, unlike men, when women say they want to do some more thinking and talk with other people, that's exactly what they mean.

It's part of a woman's collaborative nature to draw others into the process of helping her make decisions. It's also true that while men want to make a good decision, for a woman it has to be a *perfect* decision—one that meets all the many needs on her radar screen, including the needs of all the people in her life. This need may also go back to the feeling that when it comes to finance, she's on foreign territory, and can't risk making a wrong move.

Meanwhile, the salesman, at the end of a bad month, was caught up in his own perfectly understandable need to boost his sales. Unfortunately, the harder he tried, the worse the situation became.

BECAUSE MORE OF TODAY'S BUYERS ARE WOMEN?

The manager of a car dealership we work with said the percentage of clients they sell on the first visit has fallen from 21% to just over 14%.

One of the biggest lessons here is the importance of maintaining a balanced attitude.

Accept the fact that women are probably going to take longer to make a decision than your male clients. Don't think that if they leave your office without agreeing to buy you have lost them. In most cases, they will come back. If you try to force them into a decision, on the other hand, they probably won't.

You need to approach the close in the belief that it is another step in the process of developing a relationship, and not the final step, either. Instead of worrying that you will lose the sale if you don't close now, adopt an attitude of abundance: you will sell your client eventually—if not today, then tomorrow.

In addition to these "attitude adjustments," there are five specific steps you can take to keep your client in charge of the selling process so that you can make the sale her way.

1. DRIVE THE PROCESS, NOT HER DECISION

Although you cannot shorten a woman's buying cycle to meet your needs, you can guide it: not pressuring her doesn't mean you should do nothing. While she wants to make the decision on her timetable, she also wants you to ease the process for her. Again, remember that for her this not a transaction; it's a *relationship* with a trusted adviser.

Let her set the pace by asking what she needs to move forward. Maybe it's more information; maybe it's a review of information you've already provided.

What additional information can I get for you?

What's the best way to get it to you?

Act as her intermediary with other people or departments so she gets what she needs. Most of the time this is pretty straightforward: collecting more information, for example, or helping with forms.

2. HELP HER WEIGH EACH OPTION

Deciding how best to secure her future is an important decision so it's no wonder that a client might want to go slow. If she's got a lot to consider, she'll appreciate your help with comparing the various options. One approach that keeps you out of the "pushing" mode is to go back to the priorities she gave you, and show her how the options measure up.

I made this recommendation because you told me you didn't want to get involved in making daily decisions about your investments. Do you still feel that way?

Ask her to describe the risks she sees. Don't try to talk her out of them.

When you think of putting your money in these annuities, what risks come up for you?

What contingencies would you want in place to feel more secure?

Walk through the potential gains, downsides, and trade-offs of each option. Then compare the options with regard to their pluses and minuses.

Offer your best advice—when she asks for it. You may have to bite your tongue to keep from telling her what you think she should do. Try to remember that in helping her to come to her own conclusion, you're also continuing to build a relationship with her that could result in substantial future sales.

Demonstrate optimism, enthusiasm, and patience. Reaffirm that she's making an important decision and is right to be taking her time. Assure her that the approach she's taking will produce a decision she'll be happy with. Offer her your continuing support.

3. GIVE HER SOME ROOM

Many women will want some mental breathing space to think, talk with family and friends, and let everything sink in. Give her as much space as she needs. If you're meeting in your office, you might want to create a quiet spot for her to review what she's learned. Offer her the use of a conference room to read and think. Make a phone available.

At the same time, make yourself available, and be sure she has several options for getting in touch with you.

The biggest challenge in waiting for her final decision may be managing your own anxiety. Having invested a lot of your time and energy, it's hard not knowing when—or if—the deal will go through. One way to reduce your uncertainty is to have already planned what your next move with her will be. Will you follow up with some more information? Give her the name of someone she could talk to?

Suggest a concrete plan for following up. The challenge here is to structure times to talk without crowding her.

Let's put a time on the calendar to get together and see where we are, maybe early next week. What day works for you?

What's the best way to follow up with you?

Support her desire to involve others in her decision-making. Don't take it personally; it doesn't mean that she doesn't trust or respect your opinion.

Would you like duplicate copies of these articles to share with others?

I'd be happy to talk with your daughter, if you'd like me to.

4. HELP HER FINALIZE HER DECISION

Because a woman will notice if you start to shift your focus from her to closing the sale, make sure you stress the importance to you of the relationship by looking back with her over what you've done to arrive at this point. Offer plenty of affirmations that she has made the right decision. Make it clear that you have enjoyed working with her and look forward to working together in the future.

Recap the outcomes she's looking for, and how her decision will provide them.

By the time Robin's ready for college, you should have a substantial nest egg for her tuition.

Nail down any loose ends. She'll appreciate your attention to detail. Incidentally, make sure you find a graceful way to let her know what you've done for her. First, your efforts on her behalf will further cement your relationship. She should know about them, if you can let her know without appearing to brag. Also, if she's not financially savvy, she will probably appreciate learning the ins and outs of these transactions.

Express your endorsement of her decision. Many buyers have moments of insecurity and doubt after making a major purchase; this is especially true for women in traditionally male industries. Also, at some level the better she feels about her decision, the better she will feel about you as the person who helped her reach it.

I gave you a lot of information to sift through, and I think you've made an excellent decision.

5. DON'T ALLOW A "NO" TO END THE PROCESS

If she decides not to move ahead, keep the relationship open. Act as if it will continue. Don't automatically assume that you did something wrong, or that she is not interested in what you are selling. Women lead complicated lives, and there may well have been outside factors that caused her to say no.

A luxury car sales associate we heard about ruined a sale by getting suspicious when a woman he had been working with appeared to back out of a sale. She was getting a healthy bonus from her company, and was planning to use it to buy herself a car. They'd worked out a price for the car and the features she wanted. She told him she would sign the papers on Friday, when she expected her bonus check to come through.

Her check didn't arrive on Friday, so she called the sales associate to say she'd have to wait until it did. Thinking this was a bargaining ploy on her part, he started applying pressure to buy now—giving her $500 off the price, throwing in leather seats. "It made me angry that he didn't take my word," she said. "I thought we had a pretty good relationship and suddenly he's hustling me. Also, I started wondering just how firm the price was. I ended up going elsewhere."

So keep the door open. She may be feeling guilty for taking so much of your time and then not buying. Alleviate her concerns by sharing your enthusiasm for working with her in the future.

I'm sorry this didn't work out, but I enjoyed working with you and hope we can work together in the future.

Create excuses to reach out. This is where your female-focused listening can pay off. If you share a common interest, use it to stay in touch. If she said she liked a certain author, and you read a review of his latest book, send it to her with a brief note.

Some salespeople make a point of having an additional piece of nonessential information they can use as a reason for a follow-up call.

Assume that you will work together in the future, and act accordingly. Invite her to seminars you present. Update her on the policies you discussed. Include her in occasional mailings you send out (preferably from you, rather than from your company).

Finally, ask for her feedback on how you might have better met her needs.

I'd really appreciate your feedback on what I might have done differently.

Take in what she says, and use it with your other women clients. A client's honest feedback is a real gift; she's under no obligation to take the time to tell you what she thinks of your performance, so listen with an open mind to everything she tells you. Don't get defensive, or try to convince her of what you were trying to do. Just take it all in, and when she's done, express your gratitude for her insights.

Pitfalls

Closing is a high-stakes moment; any one of several pitfalls can be enough to spoil the deal.

- *Assuming she's not the decision-maker.* There's no quicker way to ruin a sale than by hinting that she might not be the decision-maker. So assume she is, until and unless she tells you otherwise.
- *Misreading her nods.* In earlier chapters we talked about the fact that men nod to express agreement, women to express understanding. As you approach the close, however, you might revert to your default understanding. So be careful: just because you want her to agree, don't assume she does.
- *Rushing her.* Anything you do to hurry her along takes away her control of the situation. It also undercuts the impression that you're focused more on the relationship than on the outcome.
- *Poor-mouthing.* Don't attempt to win her sympathy by hinting at how much you need this sale. It's a manipulation; she won't like it, or respect you for using it.

To sum up: if you can maintain a positive attitude, focus on what the client wants and on nurturing the relationship, you can complete a pressure-less close. One of the outcomes is a mutual understanding that, in terms of the relationship, it isn't a close at all, but just another step in the buying and selling process.

9 SUPPORTING HER THROUGH THE SALE

How to Provide Seamless, Nonintrusive Administration

Now that she's decided to buy, is she history? Is your mind racing ahead to your next sale? Are you looking for the earliest possible moment when you can hand her over to your assistant, or to whatever part of your company provides after-sale support?

We hope not.

We know there are companies that encourage their sales professionals to pass a client along as soon as possible so they can get back out into the fray and sell, sell, sell. Chances are these companies have never heard of the D-gene.

Once you understand the perspective of a woman client who has reached this point in her buying process, you'll understand why it's so critical to provide her with continuing support.

> **"I DO"**
>
> *When a woman makes the decision to buy, in her mind it's a little like moving from dating to marriage.*

For your client, the decision to buy represents the beginning of a longer-term relationship with you, not the end. At some level she sees everything that has led up to this point almost as a kind of courtship. Her decision to buy is a reward not only for the quality of your recommendations, but also for your attentive listening, and your willingness to "do it her way." She likes your enthusiasm, and your understanding of the uniqueness of her situation. In short, because you seem to be someone she can trust and work with successfully over the long haul, she has cast her lot with you.

Living in Limbo

This period of time between the decision to buy and the final execution of the sale is a kind of limbo—for sales professionals and clients alike. Salespeople, having achieved their objective, tend to put less energy into the relationship. From here on in, they would like to think, it's all paperwork. Clients, having decided to buy, are often surprised and sometimes confused by all the additional steps and decisions required to finalize the deal.

During this part of the selling process, your understanding of the D-gene presents you with an unequaled opportunity to provide the kind of service that will set you apart from your competition. This is your chance to build her confidence that she made the right decision. Most of the products you sell are available elsewhere. Here is where you begin to add real value in the form of the peace of mind you create for her.

BECAUSE SHE CAN STILL CHANGE HER MIND

After she decides to buy, there are more decisions to make. During this time she needs to know she can continue to rely on you. If you take your eye off the ball, you could lose yourself a client.

In other words, this is no time to slow down and relax. Given everything you've done for her so far, you can be sure she will expect a high level of commitment during this phase of the sale. She's going to be very alert to any indication that your primary focus was the sale, and not the relationship.

You need to be as energetic and committed as you were before. This means finding ways to make all transactions as simple and convenient as possible for her. Your efforts will build trust and loyalty in the short term and positive word of mouth in the long term.

1. BE HER AMBASSADOR

Even though her primary relationship is with you, in order to execute the sale she may need to work with others in your organization, depending on the type of insurance or annuity she is buying. As products become more complex, many agents are forming teams. Different team members may have different areas of expertise in terms of product or type of market. In cases of meeting multiple and complex needs, these teams can be extremely effective. These joint efforts can complicate the commission, but the results are often well worth the effort. To see that she's well treated, and to protect your relationship with her, as a team member it's in your best interest to make sure all team transactions go smoothly, and to step in when they don't.

MAKE FRIENDS WITH YOUR BACK OFFICE

The people you rely on to expedite a client transaction are often overworked and under-appreciated. If you made it a point to recognize their efforts and find ways to let them know how important they are, do you think they would give your clients special attention?

We bet they would.

If it's possible, intercede on her behalf. Can you complete a form for her that's required by another department? Does she need to submit documents to another department? Could you do it for her?

Remember how busy she's likely to be. Are there procedures you could streamline for her? Penalties you could waive? Deadlines you could circumvent? She'll appreciate your efforts to remove roadblocks and smooth the way.

YOUR CHALLENGE

The idea is to make things as easy as possible for her— without breaking the law or getting fired.

This approach is in direct opposition to the "if I did it for you, I'd have to do it for everybody" view. In fact, special treatment is exactly what women want. (It's what everybody wants, although it has a bigger positive impact on women because of what it says about the relationship.) In other words, this is where your creativity comes into play.

Here's an example of creativity in action:

An older couple we know recently married, not for the first time. In the course of setting up a new life together, they bought a house, sold other properties, updated their wills, trusts, various bank accounts—all the things you do when you're joining up with another person whose life is just as complex and many-faceted as yours.

In the middle of all this, the wife decided she needed some more life insurance (primarily to provide for her daughter, who was still in graduate school). "This was not a big deal," she remembers. "I actually found an agent in the phone book."

Thinking she could complete the transaction over the phone, she was surprised when the agent suggested he stop by her house to meet with her and her husband. Because he sounded nice and not pushy, she agreed.

"It turned out to be quite an experience," she said. "He asked for a summary of all our insurance to see if there was any way he could leverage one of the policies. My husband and I looked at each other. Summary of our insurance policies? I didn't have one, and neither did he, but we ran around and scrounged up what we could find. It was a real hodgepodge: car insurance, property insurance (on two houses), insurance on a consulting business I had almost given up, plus my husband's retirement plan from work, etc. All from different companies, of course.

"Anyway, he took it upon himself to make sense out of everything. When he came back a week later, he very patiently explained our policies and how they worked. He'd also gone to the trouble of familiarizing himself with the retirement plan offered by my husband's company, and had several suggestions for how we might distribute our retirement funds so they would last throughout our retirement years.

"My husband initially had assumed he was just doing all this to get our business, and he did sell us a long-term care policy, in addition to the life insurance I had called him about. However, he also identified several areas where we were not sufficiently well covered. Did he generate some sales for himself? Sure. Did we feel grateful that he'd taken the time to identify in a serious way what we needed? Absolutely. The point was, he'd obviously done his homework, and as a result was able to give us an overview of our insurance coverage that we'd never had before. I was impressed, and so was my husband. And believe me, we've steered several of our friends in his direction."

What else can you do to make doing business with you easier for her?

If she comes to your office, you can introduce her to other members of your team—office as well as professional staff. Explain what they do and state your confidence in their abilities and willingness to help. Show her that you respect each other and work well together as a team. She'll appreciate that.

Help get copies of documents made, if that's an issue. If a life insurance policy requires a physical and accompanying blood work, suggest labs that are conveniently located and that you know have a quick turnaround. Instead of mailing out the completed policy, why not deliver it in person, and bring along a small gift as your personal thank-you?

If you work as part of a team, explain your client's situation to other team members who might be working with her. It will keep her from having to explain herself over and over. If you include some appropriate personal aspect of her story, it will help your colleague put a face on someone who would otherwise be just a name on a list.

In addition to handling matters for her personally, here are two other actions that will let her know she is very much on your radar screen:

➤ Ask her how she would like you to contact her in the future: by phone, fax, or email, and how often. Or would she always prefer to call you? Would she like regular contact, or only as needed? It's a good idea to let her know the preferences of some of your other clients, so she knows what she can ask for.

- In a letter to her, describe the kind of assistance you can best provide, and the kind of help your assistant is best equipped to offer.

2. DELIVER COMFORT, NOT STRESS

Because most women are care-givers for other people, they'll be especially appreciative of your efforts to take care of them. Anything you can do to lighten their load will make a big difference to them, in terms of time and effort saved, as well as the psychological security that comes from knowing someone is looking out for them.

Some salespeople tend to stress the problems and difficulties involved, in order to make their efforts to help seem more impressive. It's certainly acceptable to let her know what you're doing on her behalf, but ratcheting up her anxiety level is not a good idea.

Here is a brief list of phrases that create anxiety, along with examples of what you can say instead.

WORDS THAT CREATE ANXIETY	WORDS THAT MAKE HER FEEL COMFORTABLE
I'm afraid that isn't going to work.	Let me see what I can do to make that work for you.
That's not our policy.	I'll talk to a few people, and see what we can work out. We want you to be happy.
You'll have to check with your lender.	I'd be happy to get that information for you.
There's usually a long wait.	I'll personally walk your application through our office.
We've never done that before.	Let's see if it's do-able.
You need to submit that by the 15th or it won't go through.	We can draw up the paperwork for you. Then you can approve it and we'll submit it.

There are other steps you can take to add to her peace of mind:

- A new client often does not understand the complexity of his or her policy. Relieve her mind by highlighting the important points and then sitting down with her to answer questions, and review key benefits.
- Keep items pending in her account somewhere that your assistant can easily access. Then if your client calls with a question, your assistant can answer it if you are not available.
- Be mindful of her time and other commitments. Find out if it would it be more convenient if you came to her home? To her office? If she came to your office? Most men can't imagine how complicated it can be for a woman to carve out the time for even a brief appointment.
- Anticipate problems that could arise. For example, if she likes to pay by check but travels a lot and is likely to be out of town when a payment is due, work with her ahead of time to set up a payment schedule.

If something goes wrong, make sure it's taken care of promptly. Apologize to her right away, even if it wasn't your fault. Taking personal responsibility will reinforce in her mind that you value your relationship with her and are doing whatever it takes to make it a happy one.

Pitfalls

- *Over-explaining.* Assume that she's a busy person, and limit explanations accordingly. Executing the sale may involve many steps, but unless she makes a specific request for information, she doesn't need to know all the details.

- *Losing your focus.* Stay involved. After-sale support is not something you can provide with half your brain engaged—not the kind of thoughtful and proactive help that will delight her and have her singing your praises to her friends and colleagues.

10 STAYING IN TOUCH

How to Build an Enhanced Relationship with Her and Hers

If you've been applying the concepts of this book to your women clients, by now you should be sitting on a gold mine of potential new business.

As anyone in sales or marketing can tell you, the best client is an old (i.e., existing) client —for all the obvious reasons: you already have a relationship, she trusts you, you know what she needs, etc. There is also the cost angle: depending on the industry, it can cost anywhere from two to forty times more to acquire a new client than to keep an old one.[1]

The next best client is someone referred to you by an existing client. Compared to clients developed through cold calling or direct marketing, referrals are always more cost-effective. They require less convincing, they make the decision to buy faster, they tend to generate repeat business, and they are themselves more likely to refer you to others.[2] And that's clients of both genders.

A satisfied woman client is a veritable referral machine.

A satisfied woman client is a veritable referral machine. In general, a woman will share her experiences more than a man will, and in more detail. She likes to help; if you have helped your woman client, she will need little

1 Rhonda Abrams, New Business from Old Clients, Inc.com April 2002

2 Richard Banfield, *How Referral Marketing Can Grow Your Profits,* On Track Coaching & Consulting Inc. 2003

encouragement from you to let her friends and families know what you did for her, and how you can help them.

When she shares information about you with her friends, she's engaging in word-of-mouth marketing, the most important and compelling form of marketing communication. People perceive word-of-mouth messages to be credible, trustworthy, and without hidden motives. What's more, the recipients of word-of-mouth messages typically pass them on to other people they know.[3]

A satisfied woman client is one of the most powerful—and least appreciated—generators of extraordinary sales results. Think of the complex lives women lead. Each of your women clients is a potential point of entry to several markets: family members, friends, colleagues, community organizations, and businesses.

In short, whatever you can do to sustain and enrich your relationship with her will be effort well spent, both in terms of the business she will give you and the connections she will create for you with people in her networks.

In addition to nurturing the relationship, one of the reasons we talk so much about going the extra mile for your women clients is that special treatment gives them something to talk about with other people. A woman we know went to a department store to buy her husband a blue shirt with a white collar. She'd seen one in their catalog and she knew he would like it, but the store was out of his size.

Noticing her disappointment, the saleswoman said, "If you can wait until tomorrow, I'll have something for you."

The next day, when the wife went back to the store, the saleswoman presented her with a blue shirt with a white collar in her husband's size. "That's fantastic!" said the wife. "Where'd you get it?"

3 Michael Cafferky, *Let Your Customers Do the Talking*. Dearborn Trade, 1995

"Actually, I made it," the saleswoman said. "I took home a blue shirt and a white shirt in the same style in his size. I replaced the blue collar on the blue shirt with the white collar from the white shirt. Voila! A blue shirt with a white collar."

That was years ago, and the woman is still dining out on this stellar example of a sales professional going the extra mile.

1. STAY IN TOUCH WITH HER—EVEN WHEN YOU DON'T WANT ANYTHING

Knowing how, and how often, to contact a woman client is a delicate matter. On the one hand, women are busy. They can't afford to waste time in purposeless activity, and they will resent any implication on your part that they are just sitting around. On the other hand, women like to know you're thinking about them, especially when you don't have anything to sell them.

If you've been paying attention, you have discovered points of intersection between her life and interests and yours. Each one of these presents opportunities for maintaining and enhancing the relationship: sending her a book on a subject of common interest, for example, or letting her know about an upcoming event that you think she'd like.

Also, as you know, providing for one's future can be a complicated matter. New laws may have an impact on some of your clients that they can't always be expected to keep up with. So, for example, if you've been doing some female-friendly listening, you may know that one of your clients has set up a medical power of attorney, or advanced care directive. Why not suggest that you sit down with her and her attorney and update that document to conform to the new tax laws?

BE REALISTIC ABOUT WHAT YOU CAN DO

When you're just starting out, you'll probably have plenty of time to stay in touch. As you get more clients, you may have less time. This is when small-group events can work for you— as long as they feel personal.

Women like to bond with each other. They like to think of themselves as part of your family of clients. You can strengthen this perception, along with your role of trusted adviser or financial planner, by hosting small social events (no selling involved) with your clients. In addition to sharing something of yourself to strengthen your client relationships, you're also putting yourself in the position where you can keep up with events in your clients' lives that may suggest needed adjustments to their insurance.

Some possibilities include:

- Having a holiday party at your home for your women clients. Women will like knowing your family, and watching your children grow up.
- Holding small wine-tasting lunches in a local restaurant. Encourage your clients to bring friends who might need your services. Again, no selling.

Make it clear that you won't do any selling at gatherings like these; your only purpose is to stay in touch and build relationships.

Staying in touch doesn't have to be elaborate. More modest suggestions include the following:

- Visit, phone, or send an e-mail one week after a sale to make sure she's delighted with it—and to take care of any problems that may have come up.
- Send notes thanking her for her business.
- Return her calls within three hours, and always on the same day.
- Send a monthly newsletter with items of interest to women. Be sure to add a hand-written note or something else to personalize it.

- Send holiday and birthday cards. Personalize them in some way. Hint: don't send cards provided by your company; they're the opposite of personal.
- We heard of one broker who uses different types of envelopes to distinguish between personal correspondence and more routine mailings. "That way," he claims, "they're sure to open the letters I write directly to them.

2. KEEP HER ON YOUR CALENDAR

In your initial discussions with your client, you determined the type and level of coverage she needed to feel secure. Every year or two you will need to schedule a meeting in which you catch up on any changes in her life, and how they have affected her insurance needs.

Here again, your earlier efforts at female-focused listening can pay off. As children or grandchildren grow up, will they have tuition needs your client may want to help with? Or, at the other end of the age spectrum, what about your client's aging parents? Is she responsible for them? Your client herself may be reaching the age at which she relies increasingly on her adult child or children. Is it time to start talking about long-term care insurance, if you haven't already? And wouldn't it help if you had a relationship with her children?

In addition to discussing any specific changes in her insurance needs, you should also reaffirm your interest in being her long-term trusted business adviser. Any recommendations you make should support this role.

One idea to consider is sending her an anniversary card each year to commemorate the day she became your client. Include a checklist of life changes that might prompt her to review her insurance situation.

3. ENCOURAGE HER TO SUPPORT YOUR EFFORTS

Women love to support people who have provided excellent service to them. It's the nurturing part of the D-gene coming out. In other words, you don't need to push women to send you referrals; such hard-ball tactics could even backfire. On the other hand, because she's so busy, you might need to help her focus her efforts on your behalf. Emphasize your enthusiasm for your work, and your interest in helping others:

One of the things I enjoy about this job is being able to help people like you think through their financial future.

If you know other people I might be able to help, I hope you'll let me know.

4. TRAVEL IN THE CIRCLES SHE DOES

For obvious reasons, the most effective sales professionals are usually those who lead an active and varied life, have several interests they pursue, and come in contact with people from many different walks of life. All this helps them maintain a balanced outlook on their work. It also expands the pool of possible new clients, and raises the likelihood of crossing paths with existing clients.

Here are some things you can do to express your interests, in ways that will appeal to women:

- *Volunteer.* Women do a lot of volunteer work, and are impressed by men who do the same. What types of organizations or issues would you like to get involved in? Animal rights? Domestic abuse issues? Historical preservation? Nature conservation?

- *Learn about women's issues.* Read some books. Check out some newsletters. Listen to what the thought leaders have to say. You'll get a better sense of your present and potential women clients, and you may be able to do some good at the same time.
- *Work in your community.* Find local organizations that need your help, and join them. Make it your business to stay abreast of what's happening in your area: events, theatrical programs, exhibits, educational offerings, trips. You'll soon become known as the go-to guy for clients looking for a special class, a summer program for their tween-age child, or what to do with visiting relatives.
- *Stand for something.* If, in the course of your volunteer and community work, you discover a cause or an organization you feel strongly about, develop this interest. Follow your passion, as the saying goes. In time you will become identified with this interest, and people will be drawn to you because of it.

11 SELLING TO COUPLES

How to Connect with Husbands *and* Wives

Does decoding the D-gene help you sell to couples?

Absolutely. Understanding the D-gene will increase your awareness of what the woman might be thinking and feeling, and how you can best meet her needs and make her feel comfortable.

However, there is also the other spouse to consider. Together they present some special challenges. Some of these simply have to do with the fact you're having a conversation with a man and a woman at the same time. Others are created by the dynamics between a husband and wife—some predictable, others unique to each couple.

Selling to a couple may be the biggest single selling challenge a sales professional faces. Small wonder: when you sell to a couple, you're dealing with two genders who:

- Communicate differently
- Relate to other people differently
- Take in and process information differently
- Make decisions differently

OUTSIDERS BEWARE!

For many if not most couples, money is a vehicle for relating. A discussion of money, therefore, may not be only a discussion about money. It may be an arena for expressing the emotional dynamics of the relationship.

Appearances Are Usually Deceiving

When it comes to major purchases, more and more sales involve both spouses. Even though one spouse may appear to take the lead, you cannot assume he or she is the decision-maker. This is just one of the assumptions that can get you in trouble with a couple—as a D-gene-savvy salesman we'll call Marshall found out.

Marshall's story is classic. You can hear versions of it in every industry. It started when he talked to Joy, the wife, who was doing some preliminary research into various kinds of annuities. She made it sound as if this whole exercise was primarily her husband's idea. However, with what Marshall had learned about the D-gene, he wasn't fooled. The first meeting, with both spouses around their dining room table, started out well. Joy was quiet, as Marshall thought she might be, leaving it to Art to do most of the talking. Knowing his way around a D-gene, Marshall made a valiant effort to direct his remarks to both spouses, but the husband was so much more responsive and verbal. He asked questions, made connections, and in every way indicated that he was interested and in sync with everything Marshall was saying.

Eventually, Marshall found himself talking almost exclusively to Art, even though he tried hard not to.

From that point on Marshall gave up and zeroed in on the husband, answering his questions without bothering to include Joy, talking about the local football team, and, in some unwitting male bonding, joining Art in making a small joke about Joy's lack of financial expertise.

In subsequent calls to their home, Marshall always asked to speak to Art, knowing how busy women are. However, when two weeks went by and they still hadn't made a decision, Marshall found himself on the phone with Joy, who told him they'd decided to go with another insurance person—a college friend of her husband's they wanted to help out. Marshall recognized this statement for what it was: an attempt on Joy's part to extricate herself without hurting Marshall's feelings, and he didn't try to convince her to reconsider. He realized any sale was dead in the water.

What Went Wrong?

Let's take a look at this classic tale and analyze how Marshall blew the sale. First of all, the fact that the wife didn't say much shouldn't have been a clue to Marshall. Many women will defer to their husbands in public. They may have strong opinions, they may have more technical knowledge, they may be movers and shakers in their professional lives, but in public they may feel more comfortable letting their husbands take the lead. Do they not want to appear unfeminine? Do they fear damaging their husbands' fragile male egos? Who knows? For our purposes, it doesn't really matter. The point is, a woman's reticence seldom has much to do with her role in the buying process. Marshall knew this, and if he were talking only to Joy, he might have been able to use his female-focused listening skills to draw her out and establish a relationship. Art's presence, however, threw him off.

What about Art? Why was he so much more engaged in the conversation than his wife was? Was this something he wanted more than she did? Was he more comfortable talking about financial matters? Was he the decision-maker? Maybe. Maybe he was competing with Marshall. Of course, once Marshall gave up trying to include Joy in the conversation, he and Art did start to connect, but at the cost of making Joy feel left out.

And what about Marshall's laughing at the joke Art made at his wife's expense? And always asking for Art when he called their house? How big a negative impact did these behaviors have?

It's hard to say. Our best guess is that Marshall lost the sale at that first meeting. "I liked that guy," we can imagine the husband saying later to his wife. "What did you think?"

"I don't know," she probably said. "He seemed okay on the phone, but there was something about him in the meeting I didn't warm up to."

If you think that Art will dare work with Marshall after Joy drops a remark like that, you need to go back to Relationships 101. Think about it: if Marshall makes a mistake, or Joy thinks he did, Art will never hear the end of it. Joy might not be the kind of person to say "I told you so," but both spouses would know the phrase was hovering out there.

Guiding a Couple's Buying Experience

Your goal for managing a conversation with a husband and wife should be to find a way to communicate with both of them, identify and build on areas of agreement, and avoid getting caught up in the dynamics between them. It's a good idea early in your initial conversation with them to ask each person to state the reason he or she came to see you. This will give you a good idea of how in sync they are. If they can't agree on a broad generality, chances are the discussion isn't going to get easier once you get into specifics. You don't want to underscore differences, but it will help you to know how they differ in their relative comfort levels with risk, as well as their security needs for the future.

33% of all women think their households need more life insurance.

Only 20% of men agree with them.

The Women's Market: Myth and Reality, LIMRA International, 1999

If they're in agreement now but disagree as the process continues, you can refer back to this common goal to help get the discussion back on track. For example, if the spouses have reached a sticking point over their need for long-term care insurance for his ailing mother, you can remind them that the budget they drew up was based on both spouses working for the next 20 years, which wouldn't be possible if one had to stay home to provide care.

As your discussions continue, take every opportunity to restate their positions in terms that highlight areas of agreement: "It's important to both of you to find something with a guaranteed future income," you could say, or "the bottom line for both of you is to leave something for your children."

If they agree with each other but not with you, feel free to represent your point of view. If they disagree with each other, stand back. Don't try to convince them of either position. Instead, think of yourself as an educator or a facilitator—bringing up relevant information, summarizing their positions as they evolve, and, again, always looking for areas of agreement.

Some Other Do's and Don'ts

Dealing with some couples can feel as if you're walking through a minefield, but the fact is, especially in the fields of insurance and financial services, many of your clients are couples (even if you only deal with the male half) and you will need to know how to navigate successfully. Fortunately, there are some guidelines you can follow that will help you increase your chances of success—even with the toughest of couples.

- *Shake hands with both of them.* Don't lose any sleep over the "shaking hands" issue. It doesn't matter whose hand you shake first. Start with the person who is closest to you. Don't make a fool of yourself by going around the husband to shake the wife's hand first—or vice versa.
- *Until they tell you differently, assume both spouses are equally involved in all phases of the buying process.* They may not appear to be, and in fact when it comes to finances, one spouse usually ends up doing more of the work. The question is, where does the decision-making power lie? Who has the power to kill the deal? Until you know for sure, it's easier, and safer, to assume they are equal partners.
- *Pay equal attention to each spouse.* This isn't always easy, especially if one spouse is much more responsive than

the other, but if you can't figure out a way to do it, you'll quickly get yourself in hot water. If you pay more attention to the wife, for example, she'll be sensitive to the poor treatment her husband is getting, and will side with him against you.

If you pay more attention to the man, on the other hand, she'll assume you're ignoring her because she is a woman. As we saw with Marshall, ignoring the woman tends to be a deal-breaker, although neither spouse may ever say so.

- *Think about visuals.* Use what you know about the D-gene to make sure your visuals appeal to women as well as men. Also, if you use charts or brochures, make sure both spouses can easily see them. Many salespeople have two sets prepared, one for each spouse. If you decide to do this, by all means prepare them ahead of time. If you stop the meeting to get a second set of materials, one of the spouses will think he or she was an after-thought. For your sake, we hope it's not the wife.
- *Use inclusive language when you answer their questions.* Even though one spouse may have asked a question, frame your answer in a way that will appeal to the other spouse as well. Use phrases like "both of you," or "your family." Make eye contact with both spouses as you speak. Whenever possible, create bridges back to what both spouses said. Keep the focus on both of them.
- *Beware of slipping into your male default mode.* Even though you may have mastered female-friendly listening, focusing on the relationship, and all the other D-gene skills, they can seem a little awkward when you're talking to a man as well as a woman. Some male sales professionals feel the need to let the man know they are still "one of the guys," and also that they are not hitting on his wife.

You can safely forget about these concerns; they are almost certainly all in your head. The bigger danger is connecting with him in a way that excludes her.

➤ *Never provide the husband with information or a "goodie" you don't also offer the wife.* Some car dealership service departments automatically offer a man a loaner car, whereas they will give a woman one only if she asks for it. If this happens to a husband and wife, they'll both be angry—she for the obvious reasons, he on her behalf, and also because he knows every time this dealership comes up in conversation, she's going to tell him how biased against women it is.

➤ *Never turn her down when she requests something, and then reverse yourself when her husband calls.* You don't want to leave the impression that you take him more seriously than you take her. If you won't go to the trouble to get a certain set of figures for her but you will for him, that's exactly the impression you will leave.

➤ *Don't try to psych out their relationship.* You can't. No one knows what goes on behind closed doors, but you can be sure it's more than meets the eye. Your safest position is simply to treat them both as your clients.

➤ *Never, ever, take sides.* Did you ever have a friend who told you he and his wife had separated? And you offered your support by saying, in effect, that you never liked her very much, only—oops!—to have them get back together? In a way, this is what happened to Marshall when he joined Art in laughing at his wife.

Taking sides, or appearing to take sides, which has the same effect, is easier to fall into than you might think. You're taking sides when:

- You support the husband as he tries to convince his wife to accept your recommendation.

- You correct one spouse.
- You nod, smile or in some other nonverbal way let the couple know which spouse you agree with.
- You agree with a spouse's opinion of a certain restaurant, and then discover that the other spouse has the opposite opinion.

➤ *Leave them alone.* When a couple disagrees, it's a good idea for you to retire from the scene and give them time to talk in private. In this way you can avoid getting sucked into the middle of an argument. Besides, it may be easier for them to reach agreement without the presence of a third party.

12 GETTING RICH

This book is about how to get RICH selling insurance and annuities to women, right? That's what the title implies. So is that all there is to it? Now that you've read the book, you'll be living the lavish lifestyle…buying a bigger home, driving a luxury car and vacationing with the rich and famous. Why not?

It Takes Practice

Actually, there's one more thing that's required. It's important and something you'll need to take seriously. So just to lighten up a little, have you heard the one about the visitor who approached a native New Yorker on Fifth Avenue and asked him, "Tell me, how do you get to Carnegie Hall?" Without breaking stride, the New Yorker responded, "practice, practice, practice". Okay, it's an old joke, but it makes the point. How many world-class musicians, artists, and athletes have been able to improve their performance simply by reading books on the subject?

Right. Zero. In other words, now that you've read about how to sell to women, it's time to go out and start putting what you know to work: testing the skills and concepts in this book, noticing how your clients respond, and making whatever adjustments seem necessary to get the results you're looking for. You won't change completely overnight, and you may feel awkward at first, but as these new behaviors become more comfortable, you will begin to notice positive results.

The key is to find the practice mode that works best for you. For some people, putting the concepts of this book into practice will require nothing more than a series of small adjustments. For others, it will require a fundamental shift in how they think and how they sell.

That's why in this book we have presented the principles and big-picture skills as well as individual examples of D-gene-friendly actions. Some readers will learn by internalizing the principles, which will lead them to individual behaviors more or less automatically. Others, by trying out individual behaviors, will eventually come to an adoption of the underlying principles.

On the Job

If you're serious about increasing your sales by expanding your base of women clients, there are several ways you can set up on-the-job learning experiences for yourself.

- *Go back through the book, and identify a chapter that focuses on an area where you would like to improve.* List two or three of the numbered points in that chapter that strike you as especially important. Next to each point, identify a place where you could use that skill. Try it in a real situation. Evaluate how successful you were and decide what you need to do differently the next time.

- *Find a colleague who has read the book.* Choose a skill you'd each like to improve, and make a commitment to practice. After a few trial sales situations, get together and discuss what happened. Trade advice on what to do differently the next time.

➤ *Set yourself a private goal of increasing your sales to women by a specific amount over the next six months.* During this time keep track of how well you perform the skills in each of the five competencies, and where your greatest challenges are. If you meet your goal, take a few minutes to decide which skills made the difference for you. Then set a more challenging goal for the next six months.

Me? Practice?

PLACE: *United Center Arena in Chicago*

TIME: *6:20 PM*

At 8:05 the Chicago Bulls will be playing, but now there are fewer than a hundred fans in their seats.

On the court stands a six-foot-six-inch player wearing number 23. He is standing with his back to the basket, about thirteen feet out. Next to him is a rack of basketballs. He reaches for a ball, dribbles, launches himself into the air away from the basket, turns, and shoots while still in the air. He grabs another ball and does it again. And again. Jump, turn, shoot. Jump, turn, shoot.

The player is Michael Jordan, during his last week as an active player, and he is practicing his turnaround jumper. It is his signature shot. The other players? They're nowhere to be seen. They're taping their ankles, drinking soft drinks, talking to their agents or reviewing their contracts.

Out there on the court, Number 23 continues to practice. It's been forty minutes now, and the stands are beginning to fill up, but his focus is absorbed by what he's doing. Jump, turn, shoot. Jump, turn, shoot.

If the world's best basketball player at the top of his power saw the need to practice his signature shot for forty minutes before a game, then who can say that hard work and practice are not necessary at every point in our careers, no matter how successful we are?

In this book we have provided you the skills and principles you will need to achieve success selling financial services to women. Making it happen is up to you. Like Michael Jordan, you have to want success enough to be willing to work hard. You have to keep practicing and learning. It worked for Michael Jordan. It can work for you.

13 FIRST THE MONEY, NOW THE GIRL

For Men Only

So far, we've concentrated on helping you get more money selling insurance and annuities to women. Now it's time to help you get (or keep) the girl.

Can the skills in this book also help you improve your personal relationships with the opposite sex?

You can bet on it.

If you're like the men in our workshops, you've probably already been mentally trying out some of these concepts with your wife or girlfriend. So that's how she really thinks! No wonder she drives me crazy! No wonder I drive her crazy!

We'll never forget the participant in one of our seminars who came back late after the lunch break. "Sorry," he said, "I've been on the phone with my wife, apologizing for the last 15 years."

Understanding the D-gene does not mean you have to accept the blame for everything that happens in a relationship. Nor will it smooth out every rough patch you and your significant other experience. However, it sure can clear away a lot of futile arguments.

For Stan, a California broker, his first post-D-gene interaction had to do with a story his wife had wanted to tell him the night before. Here's the dialog as he remembers it:

SHE: *Did you hear what happened to the Harners?*

HE: *No, what?*

SHE: *Well, I saw Marylou at the store today, and she seemed a little different. Some people can't hide their feelings, you know what I mean?*

HE: *Not exactly, but—*

SHE: *(interrupting) Well, with Marylou you can always tell how she's feeling just by looking at her.*

HE: *Uh huh. So what happened?*

SHE: *Well, you knew they'd been in couples therapy.*

HE: *No...*

SHE: *Yes, I told you last week!*

HE: *You did? OK, so... what happened?*

SHE: *Marylou said Doug has been expressing a lot of angry feelings in therapy, and she got frightened. Apparently Doug has a really dark side. I never thought of him in those terms, did you?*

HE: *You mean he hit her?*

SHE: *No...*

HE: *What happened, then?!*

SHE: *I'm trying to tell you!!*

HE: *Are they getting a divorce? Is that it?*

SHE: *No!*

HE: *(checking his watch) OK, look. I've got a lot of calls to return. Can we just cut to the chase here?*

"As soon as I heard myself say 'cut to the chase,' I realized we had a classic D-gene situation on our hands," he said. "I'm always telling her to cut to the chase, and she always wants to give me the details. Now I realize it's just the damned D-gene."

Understanding alone won't automatically solve issues like this, but it makes them easier to deal with because it removes the element of blame: Stan's wife is not disorganized, nor is Stan cold-hearted. It's the D-gene. With any luck, once you understand the D-gene, you can both stop wasting so much energy trying to change each other.

A Whole New Light

There are many couples who would have very little to say if they stopped trying to change each other. Spousal Change, in fact, may be one of our most popular marital pastimes—especially early in a marriage—and it's one which women seem to approach with more fervor and a greater sense of purpose than men.

In an episode of the TV sitcom Roseanne, *her sister is lamenting the fact that she can't find a man as good as Roseanne's husband.*

"You don't think he came out of the box this way, do you?" Roseanne retorts. "It took me years of hard work, and I'm still not finished."

Think of a common "issue" between you and your wife or girlfriend. To what extent is it influenced by the D-gene? If you stopped trying to change her, what could you do about it?

Here's a list to get you started:

THE "ISSUE"	THE INFLUENCE OF THE D-GENE	WHAT YOU CAN DO
HE: *What's your point?!* **SHE:** *I'm trying to tell you. Stop rushing me!*	Context is important to a woman, while outcome is important to a man.	Sit back and relax. Don't look at your watch.
SHE: *You always interrupt me!* **HE:** *I do not!*	Although women's speech patterns allow interruptions, they don't like to be interrupted. To a man, interruptions are normal parts of any lively conversation.	Zip your lip. (This gets easier with practice.)

THE "ISSUE"	THE INFLUENCE OF THE D-GENE	WHAT YOU CAN DO
HE: *If he's not punished, he'll never learn.* **SHE:** *Everything is black or white to you!*	Women tend to consider personal circumstances when making judgments. Men tend to think in abstract, right-wrong terms.	Ask yourself how you would like to be judged, and be grateful that some members of the human race may be willing to show you some mercy.
SHE: *You're not listening!* **HE:** *I am, too!*	Women look for signs of active listening—nodding, smiling, commenting, while men tend to listen passively.	Respond. Nod. Say "uh huh."
SHE: *We need to talk.* **HE:** *Can we do it later? I'm trying to watch the game.*	Women derive more of their identity from relationships than men do.	Hit the "pause" button and give her your full attention. You can watch the game later. (This assumes you own that indispensable marital aid known as TiVo.)

Share the Knowledge

One important difference to keep in mind is that your wife or girlfriend is not your client. She is a full partner in your relationship. If you want to collaborate in a serious way with a special woman in your life, she will need to understand the D-gene, too. Give her the book, and ask her to read Chapter 3, "Decoding the D-gene," and Chapter 4, "Not Until She Trusts You."

We've found that when you have conflict, a little humor often helps. Here are some humorous men-made rules for women that we found circulating on the Internet.

- Sunday sports on TV are a force of nature, like the tides, or the phases of the moon. Don't get in the way.

- Ask directly for what you want. Hints do not work, even "obvious" hints. Just say it.
- So, for example, if we ask what is wrong and you say "nothing," we will act like nothing's wrong. We know you think something's wrong, but we resent the energy required to tease it out of you.
- If you come to us with a problem, don't be surprised if we try to solve it for you. If it's only sympathy you want, make sure you tell us that. Otherwise, you might want to talk to your girlfriends.
- Christopher Columbus did not need directions and neither do we.
- I *am* in shape. Round is a shape.

After you've had a good laugh, have a good conversation. See what ideas *she* may have to deal with the D-gene. She may be eager to change a few of her own behaviors since she highly values your relationship.

Get Creative

"The only time I have ever had a man pay attention to me—I mean, really pay attention—was when he was trying to get me into bed," Marsha said. "Not just the candy and flowers stuff, but listening and being attentive and remembering what I say. Of course, then you sleep with him and everything changes."

Marsha is not the first woman to make this observation. What's interesting here, however, is the parallel she suggests to the selling process. Once a prospect is wooed and won, do you take her for granted? Or, as one woman put it, "Is it only new clients who get special treatment and better rates?"

If you take a look at the five principles of trust-based selling, you will see how directly they apply to a personal relationship:

- Think relationship, not product.
- Respect her, her time, and her timing.
- Understand her on her own terms.
- Surpass her every expectation.
- Telegraph confidence.

Think about it...to sell effectively to a woman you need to do and say things to demonstrate that:

- You value your relationship with her above any sale.
- You have confidence and competence, yet you never manipulate or hurry her into a decision.
- You consider her a special individual with unique needs that cannot be satisfied with cookie-cutter solutions. She can expect special treatment from you.
- Because you listen carefully and remember what she tells you, you understand her situation, and offer help that is best for her in both the short and long term.
- You know how to adapt yourself to her timing, along with her preferred style of communicating and decision-making.
- Whenever you can, you will create solutions that will surprise and delight her, and give her stories about your creativity and thoughtfulness that she can regale her friends with.

If you show this list to your wife or girlfriend, we guarantee she'll say, "Hey, I'd like some of that!"

Also, trying out these ideas with your wife or girlfriend is a safe way to try out new approaches, fine-tune your new selling skills, and get the kind of honest feedback you could never get from a client. In any event, once you begin to put the material in this book into practice at work, you will notice improvement in all your relationships with women—whether you make a conscious choice to apply them in your private life or not.

In the final analysis, everybody wins. You increase your sales. Your women clients form a relationship with a salesperson they trust to do right by them. And you can enjoy relationships with the important women in your life—wife, girlfriend, mother, daughter—free of those frictions and conflicts the D-gene can produce.

ABOUT MADDOX SMYE'S
HOW TO GET RICH SELLING TO WOMEN
SKILLS DEVELOPMENT PROGRAM

Maddox Smye LLC, was founded in 1993 with the mandate to help companies convert more women shoppers into buyers, long-term customers and vocal advocates. The stated mission is to "help leading edge companies close more sales by building enduring relationships with women."

Firm founder, Rebecca Maddox spent over 15 years researching and developing an understanding of what women value and how women think, shop, decide and buy. Collaborating together, Rebecca and co-founder, Marti Smye, Ph.D., renowned organizational behaviorist, used the research to pioneer a scientific approach to selling to women that consistently translates into incremental, measurable sales for a blue chip roster of client companies.

Maddox Smye's 12-week Skills Development Program is based on a one-of-a-kind, proprietary sales audit system that culminates in an individualized, confidential report on 63 criteria necessary to proficiently sell and serve women customers. With "real" data as the baseline, sales professionals attend a one-day workshop introducing the five core competencies required to become a woman's trusted advisor. The program continues with 11 additional weeks of coaching and clinics, using a wide range of technology and tools that aid participants in adapting behavioral skills and producing measurable results.

For more information on the *Maddox Smye How to Get RICH Selling to Women Skills Development System,* please visit our website at www.maddoxsmye.com.

ABOUT MADDOX SMYE'S

KEYNOTES AND PRESENTATIONS

A presentation or keynote address by Rebecca Maddox, MBA, CPA and founding principal of Maddox Smye is an effective way for your organization to gain valuable insights and information from the last 15 years of research and development that gave birth to the *Maddox Smye How To Get RICH Selling To Women* philosophy and methodology.

Rebecca Maddox has emerged as the definitive voice on gender-focused selling to women. She is a recognized member of the National Speakers Association and one of the most dynamic and entertaining keynote speakers you will hear. Rebecca speaks weekly, around the world, to audiences representing thirty-six different industries. A sampling of her keynote topics include:

How to Get RICH Selling to Women

In this interactive and energizing presentation, you will learn the five common sense principles that hold the key to building T.R.U.S.T. with women and the 5 core competencies required to close sales with women, the application of which has been reported to increase personal revenue by 45%.

To Women, You Are Not a Billion Dollar Corporation, You Are a Guy Named Dave!

Selling to women is a science, requiring both knowledge and action. Rebecca provides the knowledge— by introducing the 5-key competencies and the accompanying behaviors required to close sales to women. Your sales team provides the action— by implementing the strategies and tools from this presentation to experience immediate and significant results.

The New Frontier: From Competitive Advantage to Competitive Necessity

With women having responsibility for 89% of purchases today, if you still consider them a niche market you're already behind. Every year more sales are going to come from a purse and not a pocket in every consumer market. In this compelling presentation, Rebecca will help you position your sales force to get in the lead, close more sales to women and build the enduring relationships that result in loyalty and referrals.

For more information on Maddox Smye keynotes and presentations, please visit our website at www.maddoxsmye.com.

SHARE THE MESSAGE OF

HOW TO GET RICH SELLING INSURANCE AND ANNUITIES TO WOMEN!

WITH YOUR CLIENTS AND YOUR SALES TEAMS

To get information or order additional copies visit our website at: www.maddoxsmye.com

WRITE US AT:

300 5th Avenue South
Suite 101, Box 420
Naples, Florida 34102